TROOPER TALES:
REAL STORIES OF
CHRISTIAN FAITH
IN DAILY LIFE

BY

DANNY MOON

TROOPER TALES: REAL STORIES OF CHRISTIAN FAITH
IN DAILY LIFE
Copyright © 2002 by Danny Moon
Published by The Hometown Missionary

Editor: Linda I. Delbridge, Ph.D.
Cover Design by Dave Johnson
Author photograph courtesy of Kim Christiansen Photography

Library of Congress Control Number: 2002090592

ISBN 0-9717045-0-3

First Printing January 2002

Printed in the U.S.A. by
Morris Publishing
3212 East Highway 30
Kearney NE 68847
Phone: 1-800-650-7888

CONTENTS

Dedication

I dedicate this book to two people.

First, my big brother David.
He suffered from a connective tissue disorder
called Ehlers-Danlos Syndrome.
He went to be with the Lord at the age of 15.
Through his sense of humor and his short life,
he taught me how to make lemonade out of life's lemons!
Thanks, Dave!
We will talk again some day.

Second, my loving wife Tresa.
I met her in the eighth grade and
I have been in love with her ever since.
She has been a constant source of love and support.
She has followed me all over the country on each of
my little adventures and never complained once.
She has taught me the true meaning of love.
I list you second here only because
you came into my life after David.
You have the number one place in my heart!

ACKNOWLEDGEMENTS

There are many people I would like to thank. I will only mention a few.

The first is Linda Delbridge, my editor. Without her knowledge and support, this book would never have been sent to the printer! Thank you, Linda!

I need to also thank my chaplains, Dick Glasgow and Dick Johnson! You have been along-side me all the way! Your constant support and encouragement mean the world to me! You have taught me, by your lives, the true meaning of what it is to be a Servant!

FOREWORD

In *Trooper Tales*, Danny Moon is able to share his daily adventures and tie those experiences directly to scripture. The Bible says God simply wants our honest and sincere words. With this book, Danny has truly shared his heart for the Lord through honesty and sincerity. I believe those fortunate enough to experience Danny's book will follow his lead and work harder to apply scripture every day of their lives.

Proverbs 22:17 asks "Open your ears, and hear the words of wise people, and set your mind on the knowledge I give you." I encourage people to consider this verse when reading Danny's book.

I have had the joy of knowing Danny for more than 12 years. I remember watching him grow as a State peace officer candidate while I served as the Camp Commander during the 15th Department of Public Safety Academy. He is without question a devout Christian with his priorities rooted in God and family. His career to date has proven his dedication to the Iowa State Patrol and the people of Iowa.

My hope would be for many people from diverse backgrounds to experience God's work as a result of reading this book.

Colonel Robert O. Garrison
Chief,
Iowa State Patrol

INTRODUCTION

This book is a product of my ministry called "The Hometown Missionary" that I started in 1995 as an outreach to people of all kinds. I wanted a way to encourage people to live out their faith on a daily basis. I have found that it helps to share the events of our everyday lives with each other.

I am just a regular guy. I have my own set of struggles in life, and I have plenty of bills to pay. Like every one else in the world, I have my own calling. I am a police officer.

I am out in the real world every day. I come in contact with what are sometimes some pretty unusual situations. Because I am incredibly good at being a sinner, the Lord often has to teach me lessons along the way. I type out these lessons, some about police work and some about my personal life, to share with all of you, to let you know you are not alone in your struggle to fuse together all the little pieces that sometimes pile up in our lives. When our Christian walk turns into a crawl, it is helpful to know that we are not alone, and to be reminded that greater is He that is in us than He that is in the world, the world to which our Lord sent us to share the Good News of Salvation (Mark 16:15).

I sincerely hope you will be able to relate some of these lessons to your own personal life. I hope I am not the only one God has to work on continually! It doesn't matter what church you attend or what your background is. If you believe that Jesus is the Son of the living God, that He died on the cross for the remission of sins and rose again defeating death for all who believe for all time, then you too are a missionary in your hometown!

I pray that these stories encourage you in some way. I pray that you will find the courage to share with others. In the everyday real world, Christians who are getting beaten up need backup Christians to stand with them. Non-believers who are dying need our urgent response.

This is the real thing! Code 3, 10-33, red lights and siren!

Danny Moon

The Hard Way

Do you have to burn your hand before you know the fire is hot? Do you have a learning disability when it comes to profiting from others' mistakes?

Did your parents turn prematurely gray because of all the times they had to say "I told you so" after you rushed headstrong into another "learning" experience?

Did you have to be married for eleven years with three kids before you could admit your predominant learning style is "the hard way"?

That's me.

Even as an adult and as a state trooper, I find myself occasionally learning "the hard way" that fire burns.

The fire was already blazing one night, and I was running from situation to situation. I was handling it all and was pretty proud of my ability so far.

I was in a small town helping a local officer search for a lost child when I received a call about three drunks who needed to be taken off a bus on the interstate. They were 50 miles away, which seems to be the typical distance when I get a call. Sometimes the miles are a blessing that allows time to consider the situation along the way. However, everyone else gets the upper-hand advantage because they have time to consider what they will do once I arrive. They will know what's going on; I won't.

I asked the dispatcher to find someone closer to the bus to handle the situation until I arrived. She soon informed me that two other officers were nearby and would try to maintain control until I arrived.

While enroute, I received additional information. The on-site officers seemed nervous and anxious. I sensed trouble ahead.

They warned that the passengers to be removed would cause trouble if handcuffed. However, I have dealt with enough drunks to know it's impossible to reason with people in their condition, and so for safety reasons, I decided handcuffs were the first order of business. The on-site officers had eighteen months of experience between them which, I am ashamed to admit, made me feel important. I entertained thoughts of "showing them how it's done."

That I had controlled the fires successfully that evening and assumed I was on a roll proved to be a nearly fatal mistake.

As Proverbs 16:18 warns about learning the hard way, "Pride goes before destruction, a haughty spirit before a fall."

I arrived to find the two officers beside the bus with three drunks sitting on the interstate guardrail. The officers and the bus driver approached me to explain that one man had threatened the driver with a gun; the other two were accomplices.

I proceeded with my best "Barney Fife" impersonation, pulled up my gun belt, and approached the three drunken bandits. I would show them who was really in charge here!

I started with the first in line and asked him to get up and put his hands on the side of the bus. Immediately, he started his song about the injustice that he perceived was about to take place. I grabbed him and "escorted" him into position along

2

the side of the bus to handcuff him. I had quite an audience, so I really wasn't too concerned about the other two at this time. I figured the other two officers would handle the other two drunks. However, as I finished wrestling with drunk number one, I looked up in time to see drunk number two stand up, jump the guardrail, and run into the weeds!

I couldn't believe it! He apparently didn't get my message about who was in charge! Since he obviously had to learn things the hard way, I ran after him, caught him, jumped on his back, and wrapped my legs around his. We went down. That's when I realized this was a really big guy.

He was not impressed. I learned later that he was 6'3" and weighed 230 pounds to my 180-pounds-soaking-wet! I had done little to introduce him to my authority.

As we rolled downhill, my watch broke and my flashlight went flying. I tried my best to grab hold of this Goliath, but I understood rather quickly that this guy was a lot stronger than yours truly. We wrestled for what seemed an eternity before one of the officers arrived. I experienced only slight relief before I felt Goliath reach for my gun. He was on his belly and partially on his back. My waist was almost directly over his left hand as I tried desperately to get a grip on his arm. I could feel his hand trying to maneuver into a position to get hold of my gun.

Overwhelming fear raced through my body as I suddenly realized he was not playing games: "He means to take my head as a trophy!"

Instinctive training took over. I reached my left arm under my weapon to bring it into a position that would prevent him from removing the gun from its cross-draw holster. I continued to wrestle with him, now with one arm partially disabled. What

3

if he tried for the other officer's gun and was successful? "He's trying to take my gun!" I yelled.

With fear, adrenaline, and stress taking their toll, I grabbed a blunt striking instrument I carry in my back sap pocket and aimed at Goliath's shoulder. Other hard-to-handle fighters had complied immediately and I expected him to do so. Wrong! He laughed and mocked the other officer and me.

I was truly scared. I struck him a few more times in the shoulder area attempting to immobilize his arms enough to restrain him. He continued to resist and make fun of our efforts.

I was tiring. I heard my labored breathing and broken speech. Plain and simple, I was becoming tuckered out. Under my breath, I cursed myself for becoming complacent about workouts. Had to learn the hard way, again, didn't you.

I considered the possibility that I might have to break free and draw my gun before someone got killed: namely, me!

Still struggling, I fought to keep calm as thoughts of my wife and children raced through my mind. I had no time to stop and pray, but the Lord knows our hearts, and in His mercy, He heard mine cry out for help.

His promises are true: " 'I will rescue you on that day, declares the Lord; you will not be handed over to those you fear. I will save you; you will not fall by the sword but will escape with your life, because you trust in me, declares the Lord' " (Jeremiah 39:17-18). Peace settled around me as He appeared to show everyone exactly who was in charge.

For some reason, Goliath decided to give up. I wanted to think I scared him, but I knew otherwise.

All three men were taken into custody, and all three were quite "lippy" on the way to jail. Two were charged with public intoxication. I charged Goliath with everything I could think of: public intoxication and assault on a police officer among others. He still wanted to fight: he destroyed his holding cell at the jail. The judge reviewing the case gave him credit for time served and let him go. Goliath walked to the bus stop in town, bought another ticket, and I haven't heard from him since.

Except for those in law enforcement, most of us will never have to face physical battles like the one I experienced. But in all battles, even this one, the focus is not on the physical for it is simply the fallout or the direct reflection of our spiritual battles.

We all confront Goliaths. But because God is faithful, we don't have to be afraid to do battle with them. To be prepared, I need to maintain my physical as well as my scriptural workout schedules. Being grounded in God's promises and His word means I am well-armed when the Goliaths appear.

Even bystanders must be alert and prepared, for none of us knows when our own strength and ability will be tested. Those who think they are called only to assist must also be prepared to challenge the evil about us.

Ephesians 6:12 explains, "For our struggle is not against flesh and blood, but against the rulers, against the authorities, against the powers of this dark world and against the spiritual forces of evil in the heavenly realms."

We don't have to learn the hard way. The Lord has already given us victory, if we accept it.

For our struggle is not against flesh and blood, but against the rulers, against the authorities, against the powers of this dark world and against the spiritual forces of evil in heavenly realms.

-Ephesians 6:12

THE BUNNY

S unshine and my good mood forecast a productive day ahead. Then out of the corner of my eye, I saw something along the roadside. As I slowed to investigate, I realized it was only a floppy-eared little bunny. No big deal. I continued on my way.

About a quarter-mile down the road, I spotted a farmhouse with a swimming pool and bicycles in the front yard. The bunny must belong to children who live there.

My heart started to melt at visions of those poor little children outside calling for their little bunny. My imagination shifted into high gear. I saw the teary-eyed youngsters searching frantically for their treasured pet, weeping as they cried out, "Floppy-eared little bunny, where are you?" I imagined worried parents as they discussed how they would deal with the inevitable, guiding their children with wise words as they held their hands, and themselves aching inside as the children cried themselves to sleep.

That's right. I turned around to see if the bunny was still there. He was sitting by the side of the road. I rationalized, "If that thing is a pet, it will probably come right up to me and jump into my arms." I parked the patrol car and carefully walked up the shoulder trying not to scare the poor critter.

To tell the truth, I was trying to look as official as I could because of the traffic that time of the morning.

As I got close to the bunny, it took off like a bolt of lightning. Decision time: Do I forsake my official-looking posture and chase a rabbit up the highway, or do I walk away and say that I tried? I was tempted to walk away. Not only did

7

I not desire to make a fool of myself, but also my uniform isn't designed for track events. It won't take much for them to get another rabbit, I concluded.

But then I envisioned those teary-eyed children again. I didn't even know them, but I couldn't bear the thought of them finding their pet bunny squished in the middle of the highway. So I took off and chased the little varmint with all my might. It's a miracle I didn't end up covering an accident, considering the number of drivers who turned to see what the officer was chasing! I must have looked just like a cartoon version of one of those TV cop shows!

Over the hills, through the woods, into a muddy bean field...I finally scooped up the rabbit and returned to my patrol car, trying not to attract any more attention than I already had. I turned on the air conditioning, tried to catch my breath, and cooled down a bit. I imagined my triumphant entry at the farm. The children would come running. Tears of joy would flow down their faces as they hugged their long-lost Floppy. What a hero I would be! Making a fool of myself comes naturally, but it would be well worth it when those children saw the bunny that they surely thought was gone forever!

As I drove into the farmyard, the farmer came right out.

Wait a minute! "That's an older guy, not the worried parent I was expecting." I was a little worried myself as I got out of the car. What if he didn't own this thing? What am I going to do with it then? And what about my fame as the rabbit-rescuer?

I greeted the farmer and asked if he by chance had a floppy-eared little bunny. "Why yes," he answered. Great - all was not lost! This guy probably would miss the company of his pet just like kids would. Besides, he didn't seem to be in any shape to chase a rabbit.

As I opened the door to release the rabbit, the farmer acknowledged, "Yep, that's him all right. I've got two of them. They just run wild around here, you know! The grandkids like to chase them around. You know kids, full of energy!"

I won't write what went through my mind at that point.

But I can tell you that it doesn't matter what the problem is or whether all the facts of the situation are evident. It is always better to try and to reach out to someone in need...even if it means making a fool of yourself. If we really are "the salt of the earth" (Matthew 5:13), then we cannot afford to risk someone else filling the need that God has allowed us to see.

> Let us not become
> weary in doing good,
> for at the proper time
> we will reap a harvest
> if we do not give up.
> -Galations 6:9

Drunk with a Gun

I started the day late. I was in a hurry and my mind was filled with the many tasks I had to accomplish that night. I got into my patrol car, turned on the radio, and let the dispatcher know I was on duty just in the nick of time! I breathed a sigh of relief, still feeling that I was forgetting something. "Oh well, it will come to me later."

On to the first order of business. Coffee with the boys! Out of the driveway, to the corner. My gun belt! Back to the house. Finally ready.

I had to hurry to meet the boys. I was working 9 p.m. to 6 a.m. and the others would be getting off duty soon, leaving me mostly by myself to cover 97 miles of Interstate 80. A few county deputies would be out - the key word being "few." With a lonely night ahead, it was important to see at least a few friendly faces.

After our brief coffee break, things were going well. It was shaping up to be a routine night.

Wrong. The dispatcher reported that a county deputy, 50 miles away, needed help. A drunk had barricaded himself in his house; he was armed and threatening to shoot the deputy and himself. Another deputy from the next county was on his way to assist, but he was as far away as I was.

That comfortable relaxed feeling was gone. My blood pressure rose and the adrenaline pumped. I am not too proud to admit I was scared. I don't want to get hurt: my wife Tresa would never forgive me!

I raced toward the distressed deputy with surging emotions. I endeavored to block out the mix of fear and excitement and focus on the task ahead. First, I had to get there in time. I played out various scenarios in my mind so I would be prepared before I arrived. Even with all of these things on my mind, it suddenly hit me like a lead glove: my first order of business should have been my devotion and prayer.

Great! Add a little guilt to the mix! I sensed complete understanding of "contrite" at that instant. I was truly sorry I hadn't made time for the Lord that morning. So while driving very fast, I prayed like I'd never prayed before. I started out, "Lord, I hope you don't believe turn-about is fair play!" I wanted Him along.

I arrived at the house and found two deputies and a city officer there. They had taken cover behind a truck and were trying to talk the gunman out of the house. One of the deputies was successfully keeping the dialogue going, but the "good ol' boy" routine wasn't working. The man inside was drunk, mad, and scared. It became obvious to all of us that we weren't going to be able to talk him out.

I recalled advice from my father, the salty city policeman: "Remember, boy, it takes a good thief to catch one!" Although it was 3:00 a.m. and we were all a little drained, we came up with what seemed to be a good plan. After I had broken a back bedroom window, a city officer would hoist me into the house. Once I was inside, the deputy would shoot pepper spray into the gunman's face through the window. Like a thief in the night, I would ever-so-quietly stalk through the house to his agonizing screams, then disarm and tackle him while the other officers kicked in the front door.

We left the cover of the truck, the deputy made his way to the window safely and laid a marvelous "good ol' boy" routine on the gunman to distract him. That was my cue! The city officer gently lifted me to the window. I carefully pulled myself through. I fell onto a dresser, knocked over all kinds of stuff, tumbled to the bed, then thudded onto the floor.

(It's funny, what goes through your mind at a time like this. I know God has a sense of humor, but I really hoped this was the extent of the "turn-about" part!)

The drunk turned from his window, shouting and swearing: "Who's in here? I told you what I was gonna do if you came in here!"

I got up quickly, blinded him with my flashlight, and rushed toward him with all the speed I could muster. I wanted to reach him before he had time to gather his composure and raise his .22 rifle. I hit him with all my strength and we both dropped to the floor. By the time I got him wrestled over with one of his arms behind his back, the other officers had kicked open the door and were inside like the cavalry of old.

> For this is what the high and lofty One says - he who lives forever, whose name is holy: "I live in a high and holy place, but also with him who is contrite and lowly in spirit, to revive the spirit of the lowly and to revive the heart of the contrite. I will not accuse forever, nor will I always be angry, for then the spirit of man would grow faint before me - the breath of man that I have created. I was enraged by his sinful greed; I punished him, and hid my face in anger, yet he kept on in his willful ways. I have seen his ways, but I will heal him; I will guide him and restore comfort to him, creating praise on the lips of the mourners in Israel."
> - Isaiah 57:15-19

Thank God, He is forever faithful!

Pumpkin Pie

I t was a snowy Thanksgiving Day and I was patrolling the county highways. I felt sorry for myself as I watched people traveling to and from family gatherings while I was stuck working. I had taken a sandwich to work because not a single restaurant was open in my patrol area. I stopped a few travelers to "visit," of course. Most were happy, full or hungry, depending on the time of their family feast. Drivers didn't seem as "thankful" after our meetings, but that's my job and I did it.

[A side story: At that time, we lived in an old farmhouse that I loved. I miss the house but not all the "honey-do's" that came with it! It seemed that Tresa always had something for me to repair, improve, take care of, etc. Whatever the project, my style is to tackle it with a passion - not because I necessarily enjoy doing that kind of stuff but because I need to conquer and complete my mission. As a result, I always had all sorts of little cuts on my hands because of my lack of patience.]

As the day wore on, the snowfall grew heavier, roads became snow-covered, and travel became increasingly risky. Cars slid into ditches and I was sent to rescue passengers. How things change: one minute I was a creep and the next a hero!

Before long, the inevitable happened: I was called to a personal injury accident.

I turned on my top lights and headed for the accident site. My heart always races as I anticipate what I might find ahead while trying to find that fine balance that keeps me on the road while knowing lives may depend on how fast I get there. If I ended up in the ditch like so many others that day, I would fail for sure. Little did I know my own life would soon be in jeopardy.

At the scene, I found a little blue car with the back end mashed and another car with front-end damage. What first caught my attention though was a man running around his car with blood all over his face and chest. I parked the patrol car in an attempt to protect the scene and jumped out to find out what was going on. The man continued to scream and rant. I got closer and then started to smile: all the blood was coming from his nose. Nothing major, thankfully. He was really carrying on, hopping around his car, hollering in a high-pitched voice, his arms flailing about with his hands ending up on his hips like a furious woman! I had assumed he was ranting about his car but realized he was upset about his pumpkin pies which had been thrown everywhere.

"I just stayed up all night baking those pies, and I just don't know what I will do now! Mother will be so unhappy. Thanksgiving just will not be the same without my pies." He was so obsessed with the pies he was unaware that he was bleeding all over.

I quickly scooped up a handful of snow, packed it on his nose, and tipped his head back to stop the bleeding. I heard a muffled "Oh, that's cold!" come from under my hand.

After the bleeding stopped, I filled out an accident report, wrote him a ticket, and went on with my day, chuckling to myself a little before putting the incident out of my mind.

A month later, the courthouse clerk informed me an arrest warrant had just been issued on one of my tickets. Someone had neither paid the fine nor appeared in court. When I saw the out-of-town address, I knew that person was trying to get away with not paying one of my tickets. I was not about to let that happen. My research showed it was the pie man. I would take him a piece of pumpkin pie all right - for his ride back to jail! (I thought I was pretty clever!)

I did not know what this man's sexual orientation was but I knew what my guess was. While I do not condone the homosexual lifestyle, I do know this man was a child of God. Jesus Himself died on the cross for his sins, whatever they were, just as He died for my sins. I Timothy 1:15 tells us, "Here is a trustworthy saying that deserves full acceptance: Christ Jesus came into the world to save sinners - of whom I am the worst."

My judgment of this man, my condemnation because of his assumed sin, and my failure to show the compassion he deserved as one of God's creation made me just that: the worst.

I did not realize this on my own accord, however. Once again, because the Lord loves me, He hit me over the head with a major hammer (Hebrews 12:6).

When I called the man's house, his mother answered. When I told her who I was looking for, she replied, "He is not here at the moment. May I ask why you are calling?"

I explained who I was and that I had a warrant for his arrest. I wanted to come and get him. I asked her where or when I could find him. Her reply shocked me: "He passed away a few days ago."

He'd had full-blown AIDS.

Then I understood why he was so upset about the pies. This was to be his last Thanksgiving, his last opportunity to share his pies, and he knew it.

I thought of grabbing his bleeding nose with my hand, I looked at my hands covered with their usual little cuts, and I felt sick. "Ok God, you have my attention now!"

Sin is sin. It does not matter how big or how small it may seem: it is all the same in the Lord's eyes. I wondered if the "little" sin of pride and passing judgment would be my undoing. How often the "little" sins sneak into our lives and cause the most destruction! Sometimes they are disguised as "socially acceptable"; we don't think they are any big deal; we don't even notice them. Jesus thought they were a big deal: He died for them.

Thanksgiving had been a month ago. I was scared. If I were infected, I could infect my wife as well. Isn't that just how sin works in our lives? It's contagious, like a disease. It could take a whole family. The Lord didn't even spare the angels when they sinned (II Peter 2:4). I prayed He would have more mercy on me.

I went to a hospital to have a test run for AIDS. Just as we didn't have a protocol for handling possible blood-borne pathogens at that time, no one was quite sure what to do when I reported the potentially deadly encounter. As I awaited results, I learned my lesson about judging others. In Matthew 7:1-2, Jesus admonishes, " 'Do not judge, or you too will be judged. For in the same way you judge others, you will be judged, and with the measure you use, it will be measured to you.' " I prayed God would not hold me to the same standard to which I had held the driver I ticketed.

The tests came back negative. According to the doctor, the chance of infection was slim. But it was enough to scare me.

I learned we can love the sinner without loving or condoning the sin.

Doing anything else might be our *un*doing.

> "A new command I give you: Love one another. As I have loved you, so you must love one another. By this all men will know that you are my disciples, if you love one another."
> - John 13:34-35

GOD JUNIOR

My new partner, JR, rides with me continually during my duty day. He has a photographic memory and listens intently to every word I say. He speaks only when I allow him to and the topic of his conversation is usually centered on me. Unfortunately, JR is not a real person; he is my in-car video camera.

I call him JR because he's kind of like God, you know, always watching! God Jr. is a great benefit, most of the time. It's always remarkable how fast attitudes change once people realize they are on "Cops' Candid Camera."

As I watch the tapes, I find it very interesting to sit back and "arm chair quarterback" myself. I've noticed a variety of odd things I do without being aware, some of which can be safety issues. I have also seen and heard people do things on tape that I wish I'd noticed at the time I stopped them.

I've also realized the sensitivity of the body microphone with which I'm wired. Because the body armor and gun belt I wear can be very restrictive and uncomfortable, I've noticed that I occasionally let out a little grunt when I'm getting out of my car. I've kept my eye on that one! Kind of embarrassing, you know.

The video camera is housed in a locked compartment to ensure its integrity. In short, it cannot be taped over or edited. Once the tape has run out, it is removed from the compartment and taken to the office for safekeeping. And review by my sergeant.

One day I had just finished making a traffic stop and went to the local gas station to take care of some personal business. Back in my car, I looked at the monitor and felt my heart thump! I had forgotten to turn off the recorder when I went into the store. Although it was in the dead of winter, I felt a little bead of sweat forming on my forehead. My thoughts raced back to everything I said in the store. I didn't think I had said anything inappropriate but I figured I would rewind the tape and listen just to be sure.

I pushed the "Rewind" button and the "lock" light came on automatically. I rewound the tape to where I pulled into the store and pushed "Play." I sat silently and listened intently:

Grunt (get out of the car)

"Hi there. How are you today?" (me)

"He's the one you're looking for!" (Never heard that one before!)

"Good, then I can quit for the day!" (me)

"Can I use your restroom?" Oh, no!

The camera was aimed at the front of the store but my body mike was on, and in full force! I continued to listen in absolute horror as I heard myself walk into the restroom. I was listening all alone in my car but I could still feel blood rushing to my face as I heard the seat drop and the gun belt come off! Once the "other" sound effects started, I could only hang my shaking head in shame.

My mind focused on all the comments I would have to endure once my sergeant reviewed this one! I even had a few "day-mares" of the office Christmas party!

JR has been helpful to have around, but this is one occasion I wish he had stayed in the car!

This humbling experience served as a good reminder that no matter where we are or what we are doing, Jesus said He would be with us always, "even to the end of the very age" (Matthew 28:20).

We can't turn Him off, and He will never stay quietly in the car!

Poetic Justice

I was working one of my favorite "honey holes" on Friday night, about "drunk thirty." My nose got a workout with every encounter.

I was traveling east when I noticed a car in the north ditch that hadn't been there 15 minutes earlier on my last pass. I stopped my patrol car and rushed down into the ditch to see if any injured persons were inside the vehicle. It was empty except for a cloud of alcohol fumes billowing from the open door. I made a quick visual inspection of the vehicle and its contents and returned to my patrol car.

The vehicle was on the northeast side of a well-marked, well-lit, very wide intersection. All that plus perfect weather conditions meant a reasonably average person with any motor skill whatsoever would successfully negotiate that curve. Unless, of course, that person were impaired in some way!

When I checked D.O.T. records, I learned the male half of the owner couple had a previous record for drunk driving. I became frustrated as I recalled countless accidents involving drug- or alcohol-related offenses I've investigated. I remember all of the faces. How many times I've asked, "God, where is your justice? Why couldn't you have led me to this location 15 minutes ago so this person could get some help?" Why couldn't I have been there tonight to help this driver understand that this is not a game, that driving and substance abuse only lead to destruction? I felt anger for the innocent, and I felt pain for these people who have eyes yet cannot see. And again, I asked God why He let this one get away only to continue living in darkness.

21

I called for a tow truck and figured if I couldn't bring the driver to justice, at least I could inconvenience him a little. I also called his residence to see if he was home. He wasn't, but I asked his wife to meet with me at the scene. A short time later the tow truck arrived along with two other vehicles. The wife, the brother, a young female, and the driver! He was undoubtedly drunk, and the young female friend claimed to have been driving.

I wasn't surprised. People lie to me all the time, so I was a little suspicious. As the tow truck operator began hooking cables to the car, I questioned the female friend and the suspected driver in my patrol car. I was determined to get the truth out of these two. I sincerely hoped for a divine revelation! I threatened the young female with incarceration for leaving the accident scene and not reporting it. I issued several traffic citations in an attempt to break her alibi. Through her sobs and tears, she stuck to her story. I hoped the male had a conscience and that he would see her tears and break, but he didn't.

My suspicions possibly could be unfounded. It wouldn't be the first time I was wrong. I was frustrated and pretty tired of listening to this drunk babble and argue with his upset wife about their car and what he was doing out without her along anyway. I was ready to throw my arms up and dispose of this situation as quickly as possible. I couldn't charge the male because I couldn't prove he was really the driver; I could only charge the female with failure to maintain control of her vehicle.

It was evident the male considered himself an expert on just about everything, including operating a tow truck. He asked the tow truck operator if he could hook up the cables. The operator agreed (just to get him to shut up)

22

and allowed him to hook up a "dummy" cable. Being satisfied that all would go smoothly from here on out, he gained a new sense of confidence, so he returned to my car and began chirping at me. I was just about to put the "habeas grabus" on this fellow when I heard the tow truck winch start. We watched in amazement as the vehicle came up out of the ditch, its frame twisting like a candy cane! I know I was smiling because I could barely contain a chuckle. Like so many other times in my life, I just stood back and watched in awe as God handled the situation His way!

After the tow truck operator pulled the twisted wreck onto the roadway, he proceeded to unhook the cables and drive around to the front of the car. In doing so, his truck hit the car and smashed one of the only places that wasn't already damaged. The drunk driver exploded! He stomped up to the tow truck operator swearing and demanding that he not touch his car and that he get away from him before he got parts of his anatomy kicked! He pushed his car, intending to get it onto the shoulder. Instead, he hit the tow truck, causing the car to roll back down into the ditch!

His attitude and actions brought to mind these words of warning:

> Do not take revenge, my friends, but leave room for God's wrath, for it is written: "It is mine to avenge; I will repay," says the Lord.
> -Romans 12:19

No matter where we are in life, or what our frustrations might be, it is critical that we take time to find out what God has to say about our situation. You can be sure He has direction and a plan!

WEIRD

Join me on a small journey, a journey back to a Danny that very few people know. I would like to relive one of my fondest memories from the most awkward time of my life: junior high school!

For those of you who didn't know me then, I will set the stage a little to help you out. My mission in life was to secure an adequate mode of transportation: a red Honda moped. I was certain that this moped would not only enhance my efforts to be "cool" in spite of my nickname, but also would ensure my timely arrival for the after-school showing of "The Brady Bunch."

Oh, the nickname. My peers branded me as "the Rev. Moon." I was an awkward kid. I tried my hand in the sports arena by playing basketball. Fortunately, God led this Goliath-looking kid named Aaron into my life. This guy unmercifully pushed me around the basketball court, belittling me and crushing my aspiring fantasy of budding around with "Dr. J." At the time, it seemed that the "jock" scene would not belong to me. I will admit holding a grudge against this fellow for a long time. You see, I lost my sling shot a while back, thus ending the story of Danny versus Goliath.

I showed up for my first day of eighth grade with my hair at just the right length, over the collar of my new velour shirt and songs of Petra's new LP "Never Say Die" ringing in my head. I had a denim notebook under my arm. That's what the "cool" guys carried. There would be no fancy "Trapper" notebooks here! I was going to start this year off right!

Of course, I'm sure you can guess that the nerd in me shined through. Black stick-on letters spelled out JESUS down the side of the denim notebook. Next to the J, I had the word "Joy," E was "Eternity," S was "Salvation" and so on...you get the picture. Maybe I was a glutton for punishment...you know how kind eighth graders can be!

Well anyway, I strode into my English class to encounter something that even in my wildest dreams I never could have imagined. I took my usual seat at the back of the room. Then I saw something sent straight from heaven glide into the room. I thought for a moment that I was dreaming or hallucinating until SHE sat down right in front of me! Before class started, SHE got up to sharpen a pencil.

I know that my parents had been praying for a long time that the Lord would send me a godly woman to marry. Shamefully, I will admit that I had no thoughts of God as I watched her wiggle towards the front of the room! Life was in slow motion as she walked. Her blondish hair bounced off her pink "IZOD" shirt. The whole room lit up as she smiled. Who was this vision, this goddess? I must know!

She sat back down after sharpening her pencil. Once I awoke from my daydream, time not only returned to normal but it sped up. The temperature rose and my heart raced inside my chest. I was panic-stricken. Sitting at his desk behind me, the teacher called out her name! I saw her turn around to face the teacher—and me! The room started to spin and I suddenly felt dizzy as her golden hair whirled around. What would I do!?!

I struck my coolest pose and tried not to let her notice my big-eyed, red-faced, drooling stare! After talking with the teacher for a while, probably becoming a little self-conscious of the guy behind her staring at her, she looked at me and informed me she was going out with Aaron.

I was crushed! I had fallen in love, at first sight, with the girlfriend of GOLIATH! My heart dropped along side my head, right to the desk top. I felt her hair fling around once more, with all of the air of that unattainable shroud she wore.

"Oh God, what do I do now!?" I learned early that day that when you call on God, He shows up!

She asked, "What's that stuff written all over your notebook?"

My mouth opened but nothing came out! I was at a loss, speechless. In my mind, I could feel the vision of my heavenly goddess begin to sour towards a picture of Delilah...a beautiful enchantress with a hidden agenda, out to destroy me. Even though I couldn't speak, I held up my denim notebook so she could read the sticky black letters.

She opened her mouth as if wielding a sword and said, "You're weird!"

The sound roared into my ears as the iron pierced my chest! Right to the heart! She spun around without another thought as I sat there, a broken, defeated teenager!

It's amazing how we can never know what joys the Lord has in store if we are not listening. If we don't still our hearts and minds, we won't be able to hear because our reasoning gets in the way. The Lord's blessings are often hidden in what might seem at first to be the most unlikely of places. That's the power of our inheritance!

> I pray also that the eyes of your heart may be enlightened in order that you may know the hope to which he has called you, the riches of his glorious inheritance in the saints, and his incomparably great power for us who believe. That power is like the working of his mighty strength...
>
> -Ephesians 1:18

On the 27th day of September, 2001, "Delilah" and I celebrated our fifteenth wedding anniversary. And we are still counting!

CORKY

I was working, just doing my thing, when I received a call that Corky, a deputy friend of mine, needed a trooper. I was the closest one around for 60 miles. That occurs commonly enough, but what was he doing? Acting on a court order to remove children from an abusive household, the deputy arrived to find Dad and Grandpa on hand with no intention of letting him take the children. They were defending their home and their family with shotguns.

My heart went out to the children and to the deputy who is a personal friend. I wanted to make my best speed to the location. I've been in situations myself where I needed help and my closest backup was too far away. The minutes seem like hours, and the mixture of fear and adrenaline pound into your gut like a sledgehammer. Being all alone against what appears to be insurmountable odds is only exciting on TV and in hindsight.

My goal was to get there as quickly as I could. I went south to the interstate, activated every light I have, and floored the accelerator. During my duty shift, it's not uncommon for me to drive faster than average motorists. But with that far to go, and with a friend's life perhaps depending on how quickly I arrived, my mind focused on a number of factors, only one of which was my driving. I depend on my Co-pilot to take care of that; He promised He would never leave me or forsake me.

I was traveling in the inside lane and coming up to pass a string of semis. Intent on what was in front of them, I was ruling out hazards that were miles ahead but that I would have to negotiate in a matter of seconds. As I came up on the rear semi,

I glimpsed a station wagon in between two trucks. He could not see me coming because of the semis, and he pulled out right in front of me! I barely had time to jerk the steering wheel to the left. My car was on the shoulder and then down into the median! I could see the station wagon briefly in the corner of my eye as I passed it while traversing the center of the median. Instantaneous relief flooded over me, as I realized exactly what I had just avoided. My policeman-father's words came to mind: "You can't help anybody if you never get there!"

I enjoyed but momentary relief before I saw a crossover ahead. Even though I was slowing, it was approaching too rapidly. I just registered the danger when my car hit the embankment and went airborne! I mentioned God, but I'm ashamed to admit it wasn't in prayer.

When I landed, I hit hard, but on all fours. However, I did land a little crooked because on impact my head was thrown into the window and my seat was bent toward the door. I decided it was time to return to the straight and narrow - at least it was paved! Once back on the roadway, I again focused on the task at hand. With my head starting to throb, and sitting in an extremely crooked position, I decided it might be a good time to say a quick prayer, a legitimate one this time. I prayed that first of all it was just my seat that was crooked and not some important part of my car, as I again depressed the accelerator and headed toward my friend's location. Second, I prayed that the Lord would sustain my friend and anoint the situation, and carry me to his side. I figured I hadn't done so well on my own thus far!

The Lord answered those prayers. Once I finally arrived at the location, Corky and I were able to reason with the men and they soon complied with our request. The children were removed without incident. No charges were filed. And both the deputy and I arrived at our homes safely at the end of our shifts.

I left the situation with the nagging thought of how similar my recent experience was to that of my daily Christian walk. I will be going along full speed ahead when a hazard suddenly looms on the road ahead. Why? If the world sees us Christians stumble as we walk, how will the world ever see the Christ in us? If nobody wants to be part of a band of spiritual klutzes, then our mission here will fail (Mark 16:15). Where is the promise in that?

I need to remember that Jesus made more than one covenant. A promise we often forget and don't always promote as part of our witness is His assurance that

> "In this world you will have trouble. But take heart! I have overcome the world."
> -John 16:33b

Christ never promised that following Him would be void of sorrows or troubles; He did promise to be there with us when they come.

It's not the lack of falling down that displays the Christ in us; it's the getting back up!

THE CHASE

Have you ever found yourself in a situation for which you weren't quite prepared? Something comes up, you have to make decisions, you have to take action, and you find yourself wishing you'd had a little forewarning.

That's exactly where I found myself recently. I was working nights and early in my shift I was called to cover an accident. Two people were killed, so I took my time gathering all the required evidence from the scene, making certain that I did not miss some small detail that might be important.

I finished at the scene and headed to the office without taking time for supper. It was getting late and I was a little stressed already, not to mention hungry. I got to town and went to a drive-through to get a burger. I planned to take it back to the office and "sit beside some still waters" and do a little "soul restoring" (Psalm 23) before I went back to work.

I could feel the warmth of my long-overdue dinner when my radios started to chatter about some police department in a pursuit. I didn't catch where they were so I didn't pay much attention. I was just enjoying the dinner aroma dancing through my car. How often, once we think we are safe and comfortable, God steps in and halts that nonsense! You know - something about making us grow? Just then I saw a police car, its red lights blazing, come over the hilltop. In my rear view mirror, I saw him slide into a U-turn just as a pick-up truck tried to take the paint off the side of my car.

Well, so much for dinner! As disappointed as I was about changing my plans at the last moment, this was one of those times I had to play the hand I'd been dealt. I picked up the mike to answer the city officer's call for help as I floored the accelerator. I gained a clearer picture of what Pentecost must have been like for the apostles. The adrenaline surged through my veins just like the "blowing of a violent wind" (Acts 2:2).

I was right behind the pickup. The city officer soon caught up to us and advised me that they had been out on a traffic stop with this driver and discovered he had outstanding arrest warrants in two counties. Once the driver heard the "good news," he stepped on the gas, swung the truck around, and tried to run over the officers on foot, injuring two of them. For being caught completely off-guard, I was sure ready to deal with this hombre now!

He was driving about 80 mph as he turned into a residential area of town. He weaved from side to side in an attempt to keep me from getting in front of him. I was getting a little nervous. This guy was acting like he had been sent on a mission to kill someone and God had put me right behind him. Under my breath and through the radio traffic, I whispered "Thanks, Big Guy!" I prayed for Solomon's wisdom and Joshua's courage. And I begged Him to not delay the answer like He does with some of my other requests!

Thankfully my mission was clear. I had to stop the pickup driver before his mission was successful. Knowing a "T" intersection loomed up ahead, I quickly decided that is where I would make my stand.

As he slowed and chose which direction he would take, I stepped on the gas and rammed his left rear with my patrol car! The truck spun around 180 degrees as the driver slammed the transmission into reverse, backed up onto the curb, and started to take off again! I couldn't believe it: this guy didn't get enough.

So with French fries and my big roast beef completely molested, I drove up onto the curb, steered hard to the left and rammed him again! His vehicle was pushed up onto a front lawn and disabled. Before he had time to get out (I certainly didn't feel like a foot chase on an empty stomach!), I was into the passenger side of his truck formally introducing the driver to my partner, Smith-Wesson.

We got him apprehended and found him a ride to the jail. I felt pretty good - I may have been caught half asleep but at least the good guys won this time. I was standing there on the lawn feeling proud of myself, when I looked up and saw whose lawn it was. All victorious feelings drained when I realized I had chased the pickup driver and rammed him right onto the front lawn of my sergeant's house! My mouth dropped, my knees shook, and sweat beads formed on my forehead as I looked up to find him standing there resembling God on judgment day. I sure wasn't ready for this! But like it or not, I had done what I thought was right. I knew that my actions would soon be scrutinized, re-evaluated, and second-guessed by many, but not quite *this* soon.

I have been trained and prepared for just such situations. Because of the nature of police business, all officers know that life and death situations can arise at any moment. Procedure and regulations are drilled into each of us in preparation for that single instant when our lives and the lives of those we have sworn to protect will depend on how well we react before it's too late.

I would challenge each and every one of you to study your regulations and re-evaluate your procedures. There is coming for each of us an instant in time when we will stand in a situation we did not expect with no more time to study, no more time to stop and try again. Will you be ready?

"Behold I come like a thief! Blessed is he who stays awake and keeps his clothes with him, so that he may not go naked and be shamefully exposed."
                    -Revelation 16:15

THE PROSTITUTE

A hot summer night...and I was driving around the scenic countryside looking for "evil doers" who needed to bring some "judgment upon themselves" (Romans 13). Being the nice guy that I am, I always try to be available to lend a helping hand.

I had my police radio as well as my scanner on, just in case my other radio missed something. Back then, I also kept my CB on most of the time so the truck drivers would keep me informed of my exact location. I didn't know my way around all that well and they are quite attentive that way, bless their hearts. Anyway, I was feeling a little down because I hadn't had much success in my service for the night.

I was just about ready to give up and head toward the nearest coffee shop when I heard a little voice on the CB radio. A woman was getting all the lonely male drivers chattering in a big hurry. She asked if anyone out there was interested in a "date."

What a pathetic practice! This poor lady was either really desperate or really ugly, or both! Out of curiosity, I kept listening. It sounded more like she was making appointments instead of "dates"! After the initial shock wore off, it didn't take long for this naive little Christian boy to figure out that these dates would cost money!

Thank you Lord! I found my "evil doers" for the night and based on the way they were talking, they were certainly asking for judgment. All I had to do was catch them.

The problem was that with the CB, everyone broadcast my location. I would have to make a quick entrance and know exactly where to look once I got there.

I decided the best way to handle this was to make a "date" for myself. I have never pretended to be a perfect person let alone a perfect Christian, but I have never made a "date" with a prostitute before! (Mom, you can put your mind at ease.) So this was going to be a task that was easier said than done! What should I say? I didn't want to sound like a "cop" - that would blow the whole thing! It would be hard enough to sound like a truck driver let alone a lonely guy looking for a date. I needed some help! Out of habit, I bowed my head. I caught myself for a moment and wondered I if was the only guy in history to pray for the Lord's guidance in how to pick up a prostitute!

As ridiculous as I felt, I said my prayer hoping the Big Guy was in a merciful mood! I took my leap of faith, donned my best lonely truck driver voice, and picked up the CB mike. I successfully made my date with the young lady. We went to another channel and she told me which truck she would be in and what time to be at the rest area. I guess I am a better sinner than I give myself credit for.

Another trooper and myself made our appearance quickly as the mass exodus of trucks were leaving the other side. Funny how they all got done with the "potty" at the same time.

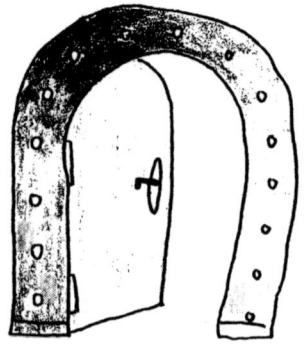

I drove to the appointed truck and climbed aboard. Inside, I found a young gal and the truck driver looking at me with the biggest sets of eyes I have ever seen! That was a good sign we had taken them by surprise! They started with the stories and the lies. We knew better. We found the man she claimed was her "boyfriend." I guess you would call him more her "manager," really. He was sleeping in his black Cadillac and vowed that we had made a terrible mistake! He told her that he would have her out of the county jail before the night was over, which would be in about three hours. We took her to jail and broke off the rest of her appointments.

It doesn't matter the kind of situation in which you find yourself or how bizarre it might be, the Lord will be there for you. Don't neglect to ask; and then remember to listen!

> "And you, my son Solomon, acknowledge the God of your father, and serve him with wholehearted devotion and with a willing mind, for the Lord searches every heart and understands every motive behind the thoughts. If you seek him, he will be found by you..."
> -I Chronicles 28:9

The young lady was released from the county jail after about four months of waiting on her "boyfriend" to come and get her. After being given credit for time served, she walked away.

TAINTED FOOD

T he day had been pretty good so far. I had just dropped off a customer at the county jail and felt the urge to put some air in my "spare tire." I called a couple guys working in the area who said they would meet me in a little town out in the country. As we gathered in the parking lot, people inside turned their heads in our direction. Maybe people usually only see one officer at a time, or maybe they don't get out much. In any case, my fellow crew-cuts and I entered the restaurant and scoped out the tactical corner booth. As we started to visit, our attention was drawn to a group of people seated conveniently on the other side of the room.

It's pretty easy to tell when people are talking about you as they casually look your way and speak in low voices so you won't hear what they are saying. I was always taught to watch the guy who is watching you, and that's exactly what we all did. These characters looked kind of rough around the edges, so we wondered which one of us had taken which one of them to jail and for what reason. We casually laughed among ourselves and joked about the kind of grudge they may hold for us because of our job.

The waiter brought water and menus. We all recognized him immediately. Last time I knew, he was doing time in the pen for drug charges. He must have just gotten out. He was in the front so we weren't too concerned about our food (usually we eat fast food and order something already in the bin). As soon as our order was posted, silence surrounded our table. Without fear of social compromise, all our heads turned to see three of the "longhairs" from the other side of the room don their aprons and head for the kitchen.

38

My stomach turned and I wanted to let some air out of that tire I mentioned earlier. We all tried our best to give each other that reassuring glance that "They wouldn't dare," knowing inside that they really might.

Our orders were served. I looked at my plate and thought of what could be concealed in scrambled eggs. I immediately kicked myself for not ordering a cold sandwich—no mayo! I knew my fellow crew-cuts had similar thoughts, especially the guy who ordered beef stew. Being macho by nature, none of us was going to cave first, so we looked at each other silently as we inspected our food and choked it down.

In the book of Matthew when Jesus gave the "Olivet Discourse," He warned us to be equally as cautious of the spiritual food that we digest. We must always look to the scripture and to the teacher sent from heaven (Acts 2) to verify the inspiration of the words we hear. Before we digest them into our spiritual system, we must be certain they are not contaminated. Take no chances!

> "Watch out that no one deceives you. For many will come in my name claiming, 'I am the Christ,' and will deceive many....and many false prophets will appear and deceive many people."
> -Matthew 24:4-5, 11

We often assume that when God teaches us a lesson, even though we know better, that lightning and thunder will accompany it. I can't help but chuckle when God chooses to teach me something without all the drama. After all, it is the simplicity of God that amazes me most.

When I'm not on some kind of special assignment, my job is to just drive around and look for unsafe driving habits of others and then bring these habits to the attention of the driver, in one way or another. Most of the time it is pretty routine, you know…the kind of stuff lessons are made of. This was one of those days. I was free from assignment and free to roam the countryside at my leisure. I was in a good mood and was a little tempted to just enjoy the sunshine when the radar numbers caught my attention. The approaching car was going just a little too fast for me to let the driver go by without a kind "how-do-you-do" from me.

I turned on my lights, turned around my car, and pulled up behind the driver. The violator and I watched each other intently as I approached the vehicle. I got to the rear of the violator's car when I noticed it was a female moving in a peculiar manner. I arrived at her window to find her hysterical.

This was not the first time I had encountered an hysterical female, so before I said anything, I thought to myself, "Oh great! I don't need *this* today!" My head dropped and every ounce of enthusiasm drained out of me. I could almost feel it puddle around my feet. I took a deep breath and painted on my best "here we go" smile and said, "Hi there. How are you today?"

My question was met with a sob. She was shaking and heaving in a convulsive nature. Tears flowed as she said, "I'm so nervous. I've never been stopped before." She tried frantically to find her driver's license. I tried calming her down a little and I tried to get her mind off of the task at hand, but all of my attempts were futile. She just continued to sob and shake and explain to me that she was so scared and that she was on her way to the nursing home to visit her crippled mother who wasn't doing well and she was thinking of her and not really paying attention.

Now that I think about it, I'm surprised she got all of that out, considering the way she was carrying on. Finally, she found her driver's license and handed it to me. I thought she was starting to calm down a bit. She was still crying, but the heaving and rocking had stopped.

As I took her license back to my car, I looked at it. I had to decide what to do. I really felt sorry for her; she was very upset. I thought, "If I let her go with a warning, who's gonna know? As upset as she is about getting stopped, I would think she would be very careful not to speed again and that, after all, is the intent of a citation, right? To get people to pay attention to what they're doing? So if I give her a warning, a little talking to, when she is already petrified, I will accomplish the same end, right? But if I do that, is it fair to all the other people that I have stopped at the same speed and given citations to? No! So it may or may not accomplish the same end, but who am I to judge that? It wouldn't be right to warn this lady and issue citations to other people at the same speed. So if I am to treat everybody the same, I need to fill out a long-form citation and impose a fine on this lady."

I've been there before and that is not a task that I looked forward to. And to be honest, part of me said, "Just give her a warning and get rid of her!"

How many different women can you find within this one drawing?

But the easy way isn't always the right way. So feeling like a heel and a dirty rotten scoundrel, I filled out the citation to the hysterical female on her way to visit her crippled, and by now probably dying, mother in the nursing home.

So like the cold-hearted jerk I felt like, I grabbed my ticket book, tucked my tail, and slithered up to her car door. I found her in the same condition as when I left her, except when she saw my ticket book, the convulsing started again. The tears rolled, the head bobbed back and forth, and the arms waved over her head like she was going to faint. If I didn't already feel like the snake that gave the fruit to Eve, I sure did now! Very meekly, I explained that I had a citation for her and I needed her signature.

As she reached out her shaking, tear- and sweat-soaked hand for my ticket book, I tried to reassure her a little by explaining that I had made the ticket out so all she had to do was send the fine through the mail. Instantly her hand stopped, her face went blank, and her mouth crinkled up. For a moment,

I felt a flash of heat on my neck as the tension changed. What did I do? Is she going to faint? Maybe she had a bad heart and I had done her in? Whatever it was, the mood of this stop changed with the speed of light.

As I bent down to get a better look, I saw red filling her face just like in the cartoons. But instead of the teary-eyed woman I was speaking with moments before, the puppy dog look changed to that of a werewolf in a horror show! She clawed the ticket book from my hand and growled out, "So this is gonna cost me, huh?"

Somewhat amazed that this second personality had surfaced so quickly, I tried to force down a smile as I replied cheerfully, "Yes ma'am, it is!"

She scribbled her name on the bottom of my citation and started to take a healthy chunk out of my hind end as she threw the ticket book at me. Now being fully reassured that I had made the correct decision in the first place, I mustered enough tact to explain to her how to send in the fine. I felt all the cracks in my face well up as I turned around and headed back to my car, smiling from ear to ear.

The single thought in my mind came from what I've heard my father speak so many times: "You can't judge a book by its cover." Did he strike gold on that one!

I learned a valuable lesson on judging others. And about judging trees by their fruit.

> "Watch out for false prophets. They come to you in sheep's clothing, but inwardly they are ferocious wolves. By their fruit you will recognize them."
> -Matthew 7:15-16

SIMPLE FAITH

Those of you who have never met my wife Tresa must know that she a vision of purity and innocence. I grew up with Tresa in a literal sense (No, she's not my sister or anything like that!). I met her in the eighth grade and fell in love. I have loved her ever since. When all the other kids were sowing their wild oats and pressing the limit, Tresa did the bold thing and declined like the good girl she was. She had an early pattern on "say no to drugs" that extended to almost everything that is an "acquired" taste. This was somewhat attributable to her upbringing and somewhat simply because it wasn't her style. The outcome is that her innocence has never been compromised, until now!

My young beauty is starting to feel the toll of having twin daughters and a son who is "a chip off the ol' block." I know it has to be the kids because being married to me for fifteen years couldn't be that stressful! In any case, Tresa recently found it necessary to indulge herself each morning in a little "pick me up," if you know what I mean! It's hard to believe, but Tresa finally joined the rest of us, the ranks of poor, weak fools who find it necessary to have a cup of coffee in the morning to get going!

With that in mind, my lovely bride went out to find a coffeepot. Having never before shopped for a coffeepot, she returned to her pre-marital habitat (the mall) to find this life-giving wonder. I came home that evening to find a new addition to our kitchen counter. I noticed this Java-making marvel the instant I entered the kitchen, largely because there was no way it could be missed!

I stood for a moment in utter amazement. Tresa walked in, caught me staring at it, and being proud of her find, was anxious to know what I thought of it. I simply replied, "What is it?"

That was apparently the wrong thing to ask. She got defensive and started to explain all the marvelous things that this new coffeepot could do! She was under the impression that the space this coffee factory took up was well worth the sacrifice. It had a fancy filter, its own water filter system, and any variety of "fu fu" coffees which could be selected by simply turning the knob. One needed not even go to the trouble of measuring the coffee: the machine did that, too! I had little choice but to give it a try.

I must admit that the first two mornings, it brewed a pretty good cup of coffee. Just good enough to make me think I was being pretty simple-minded about the whole thing.

The third morning, I awoke to a very upset wife! I came downstairs and found Tresa wearing a face that resembled my dad's when I missed my curfew. I didn't even get a "Good morning" out of her before she asked me, "What did you do to my coffee pot?!"

"I didn't do anything to it!" I answered.

Like most addicts when they don't get their "fix," she wasn't being very reasonable. It must have taken an hour of smooth-talking to get her to believe I did not commit some heinous act of terrorism against her new coffeepot. I was, however, able to hold back a chuckle when we came to the conclusion that this fancy coffee pot had simply died on its own! It lived a very short life despite all its grandeur.

We took the pot back to the store where we bought it because Tresa was convinced that it was just a fluke. It was reasonable to assume that we just got a defective coffeepot, so we exchanged it for a new one. We hauled it to the empty space on the counter, confident that our mornings would nevermore be filled with sleepy eyes and yawns. Rather, the fresh aroma of coffee "fu-fu" would fill the air.

It saddens me to report that less than a week later my beautiful bride's dreams were shattered once again. She awoke to find her beloved new coffeepot hissing and moaning. It too was taking its last breath! Once again we went to the store, this time to exchange the fancy coffeepot for a $10.00 "sale" model.

I'm happy to report that the "cheap" coffeepot has worked wonderfully for months now, despite its simplicity!

Dying along side Tresa's coffeepot was part of her innocence. She was forced to the harsh realization that "The more sophisticated the plumbing, the easier it is to clog the drain!"

Like the coffeepot, it is very easy to sophisticate our theology and complicate our faith to the point where it is almost unrecognizable. Maybe it's human nature. Another group of people tried to make things complicated: They were called the Pharisees.

Hearing that Jesus had silenced the Sadducees, the Pharisees got together. One of them, an expert in the law, tested Him with this question:

"Teacher, which is the greatest commandment in the Law?"
Jesus replied: " 'Love the Lord your God with all your heart and with all your soul and with all your mind.' This is the first and greatest commandment. And the second is like it: 'Love your neighbor as yourself.' All the Law and the Prophets hang on these two commandments."
-Matthew 22:34-40.

Maybe Jesus was really a plumber, not a carpenter.

Jesus, the Disc Jockey

I was instructed to head toward a small town and a small house from which it was suspected a drug dealer was operating. Area officers had a search warrant and I was to assist. My blood pumped a little faster as I got the call. Dealing with unknowns is pretty common in this "ministry," but with these situations, the potential for major trouble always exists. I had done this before, so I started playing out scenarios in my mind.

We gathered at a neutral location away from the residence so that we would not be seen. We had to form a make-shift entry team and decide on a course of action. After studying the floor plans of the house, each officer was given an area of responsibility. We proceeded to the house and then quickly surrounded the front door. Many of us prayed silently, then our weapons came out and the shouting started. We kicked open the door, rushed into the residence, and started "escorting" people to the floor.

Once the confusion subsided, so did the adrenaline. I looked around and wondered why anyone would want to live this way. The house was in complete disarray. My dog took better care of his house than this. I looked at the floor and my heart jumped! My chest tightened and my stomach got that sinking feeling. This house was full of teenagers! These kids were barely old enough to drive but old enough to feel that desire for "the search" (Amos 8:12 and 5:4). We all have it, and these kids had been badly deceived (2 Thessalonians 2:11). "The search" took them to all the wrong places.

A young female on the floor with her hands restrained behind her back had no idea what was going on. She babbled nonsense. My heart ached when she couldn't even tell me who she was! My thoughts went to her parents. I wondered how they would feel once the news got to them.

I looked next to her and saw an older female, the mother of one of the males also on the floor. She had been doing drugs with the youth and making a little money on the side, at their expense. I became angry with her. Even though I could not understand, it became very apparent to whom this world belonged!

We finished our search of the house and got the drugs and paraphernalia cataloged. We put the youth and the dealer-mother into our cars. I transported one of the males. As he sat in my car, his bad attitude about police officers was obvious. I sat and watched him decide how he was going to handle this situation. He seemed to think this would be a big plus for his reputation and he tried very hard to be "cool" as he sat next to me with his hands behind his back.

He spoke in a feeble attempt to make me feel like a bad guy. I had ruined their party, messed up his and his other friends' plan for the young female, not to mention that we had taken all their drugs! What a sorry soul he thought I was!

I silently asked God to help this young man. He was just beginning "the search" and he was already filled with "the lie"(2 Thessalonians 2:11) which he apparently believed with all his heart.

As with most people I take to jail, I made him listen to Christian radio all the way there. It's called a "captive audience." After he stopped telling me what a pathetic excuse of a human being I was (of course, not in those exact terms), he became quiet and began to listen to the music. He started to be-bop his head to the

contemporary beat, and then he heard the lyrics! I could see wheels spinning inside his head. This was, apparently, an unexpected twist to his new adventure!

He listened in silence for a long time. I slowed down a little so he could "savor" the moment. He spoke, but this time he wasn't cursing at me. "You know, I used to go to church." He went on to explain that after his parents parted, life went downhill. The pain I felt for this young man began to lift as I listened to his story. God is His word (John 1:1), and His word comes to us in many different ways.

Sometimes it's best to just be quiet and let Him do the communicating by *any* means He chooses! Through the radio, the Lord reached out to this hard-hearted young man and reminded him of the past. He poured water on a seed planted long ago.

Sometimes we forget the awesome power of the Lord. The Master Grower does not *need* our help, but sometimes He *allows* us to help Him in the garden.

> "[S]o it is with my word that goes out from my mouth: It will not return to me empty, but will accomplish what I desire and achieve the purpose for which I sent it."
> -Isaiah 55:11

TRIAL BY FIRE

S ometimes it can be very annoying, although it's not really that big of a deal. In law enforcement, a time comes when all officers have to sit through what is called a "suppression hearing." At a suppression hearing, the prosecution, the defense, and the judge get together and in effect put the officer on trial for catching the defendant committing whatever offense he or she was charged with doing. The intent is to see whether the arresting officer was operating within legal parameters at the time of the arrest. If the officer has built his case upon a "sure foundation," there shouldn't be a problem.

One of the first suppression hearings I had to attend came shortly after I moved and started my current assignment. I put on my funeral shoes and a clean uniform and headed off to the courthouse to meet with the county attorney. Once I arrived, we visited for a while and then went into the courtroom. While I didn't know what to expect, I wasn't too worried about it.

After all, I'm one of the good guys! I had taken a drunk driver off the road, maybe even saved her life or that of someone else. All for the good of the cause, or so I thought.

Things went pretty well at first. The prosecuting attorney asked me to describe what happened. I told him in a nutshell that I had a truck stopped on the highway for speeding and while I was "visiting" with him, I heard another truck driver call me on the citizens band radio (CB). He stated that a four-wheeler (a car) behind him was all over the road. He added, "I think he must be on drugs or something!"

I could see the truck coming up behind me fast, so I had to move quickly. I told the trucker to slow down and I would get out and try to flag the car down on foot. I told the stopped driver that it was his "lucky day" and turned him lose to take care of other matters.

Many reasons could account for why this car was weaving: health problems, the influence of drugs or alcohol, playing with the radio, or maybe just lack of sleep. In the event a female was driving, she might be "checking her look" in the mirror. In any case, you don't want to fool around when you are in control of a two-thousand-pound piece of metal hurling down the highway at 55 mph. So I thought it was important to get the driver stopped as quickly as possible.

The truck slowed down, I motioned for the car to stop, then approached the driver to find out what the problem was. The female driver was in fact drunk. I placed her under arrest and took her to jail.

The prosecuting attorney asked me a few more questions and he was finished.

Then it was the defense attorney's turn. I looked over at him. He looked like a pretty smooth customer. It made me a little nervous because as he walked up to the "Hot Seat," he flashed me his pearly whites and laid a big grin on me. You know the kind...the kind that says, "I've got something up my sleeve and I can't wait to lay it on you!" He started asking me questions and doing a little preaching of his own.

He focused on whether or not a CB radio complaint of poor driving by itself gave me the right to stop a vehicle or check something I had not personally observed.

I started thinking, "Who does this guy think I am? Some kind of communist, out driving around with no other purpose in life but to violate other people's rights? That's what I'm here for! To protect those rights. I have been called and chosen to be 'An agent of God's wrath' (Romans 13:1-6), and to uphold the laws that God Himself has established. Godly and ungodly laws are all established by our Lord and have a divine purpose."

I knew the defense lawyer was only doing his job, that is, to keep me honest, but it is very uncomfortable to be put on trial for doing what you "think" is the right thing to do at the time. I started to sweat a little. It was as though someone was playing a joke on me and had suddenly turned up the heat! In the back of my mind, I could almost visualize the flames. I had no time to look things up in the "Good Book": I had to act, and this "smoothie" didn't even mention that part.

However, he did make me re-evaluate what I had done and question whether it was the right thing or not. I was new back then and a little insecure about my responsibilities. That alone was enough to make me second-guess myself. I still thought I was right, but I also could see that the defense attorney might have had a good point. I just hoped the judge didn't see it that way.

As it turned out, the judge ruled in my favor. Over the years, I have found that when law enforcement officers act in good faith on behalf of the public good, the courts usually grant a wide berth.

But the experience made me realize that even though I have studied the "Good Book" and have been "ordained" by the appropriate legal body, there will still come a day when all of us - including me - will be held accountable for the foundation on which we build.

As a Christian, it is easy to remember that I am a child of the living God, forgiven and free from sin. But it isn't always so easy to remember that because I wear His "badge," one day I too will be held accountable for my actions.

> ...each one should be careful how he builds. For no one can lay any foundation other than the one already laid, which is Jesus Christ. If any man builds on this foundation using gold, silver, costly stones, wood, hay, or straw, his work will be shown for what it is, because the Day will bring it to light. It will be revealed with fire, and the fire will test the quality of each man's work. If what he has built survives, he will receive his reward. If it is burned up, he will suffer loss; he himself will be saved, but only as one escaping through the flames.
> -I Corinthians 3:10b-15

Mr. Confused

The night started out like many others. I was assigned to work a midnight shift on the interstate, a shift I despise! It was cold and dark and I was tired. As my family was settling into bed for the night, I was in my patrol car praying for energy. After reminding God that I was only doing this in answer to His call, I saw a deeper meaning to Paul's words in I Corinthians 1:18-25 - The wisdom of God is often foolishness in the eyes of men (my paraphrase). At that moment, I was assured that the words printed in my Bible were truly inspired, for I myself could see no wisdom in this whatsoever!

Being a faithful soldier, I donned my shield of faith and started out on "the hunt." As the night progressed, I felt more revived with every encounter. As soon as I got "in the mood" to serve God, I met *him*, John Doe.

He was in his car on the inside shoulder of the interstate, and appeared to be broken down. I pulled in behind his vehicle and turned on my lights and directional arrow. I got out of my patrol car and started to assess the situation. As I approached the vehicle, I observed only one male occupant who wasn't moving. When I made contact with him, he was alive but very confused. He did not know where he was or how he had gotten there. He didn't even remember his full name. His speech made me wonder whether or not he would be able to communicate that information even if he had remembered it. One of the only things he communicated effectively was that he had to go to the bathroom.

My mind was preoccupied with trying to ascertain who this guy was, what he was doing here, and because he was in no condition to drive, what to do with him. Most males don't have a problem with "taking a tinkle" on the side of the road; in fact, I find them doing it all the time. I told him to step into the median, where he would be in plain view but safest from the traffic, and take care of his business. I watched him walk in front of my patrol car and into the median. Instead of doing the expected, he dropped his trousers to his ankles. As truckers sounded their air horns and their high beams lit up the median like a baseball diamond, I remembered the driver saying, "I have to go the bathroom" and not "take a tinkle." After the

surprise wore off, I realized he had nothing with which to clean himself. Once the thought entered my mind of him returning to my car and sitting next to me in his condition, I decided it was time to pray! If anyone felt like they were "in chains" for the sake of the call, it was *me* at that moment!

I still hadn't had made any progress in my quest to ascertain his identity. I was tempted to call a tow truck and drop "John Doe" at the nearest psychiatric care facility and wash my hands of the situation as quickly as possible. But my "guts" told me to be a man about it and trust God to reveal His purpose.

John Doe pulled up his trousers, returned to my car, and sat down next to me (smelling as bad as I thought he would). I was once again reminded of the passage in I Corinthians 1:18-25 about the wisdom of God being foolishness to men. I was already feeling mighty foolish. Even though "the incident" was over, the truckers continued to talk about it on the CB and the air horns did not quit until we left. I hoped the wisdom of God would start prevailing any second.

Once again God was true to His word. By tracing the license plate on John Doe's car, the dispatcher informed me of a manhunt earlier that evening in a county two over from my location. What appeared to be some "kook druggie" who had taken a bad trip was really a poor lost soul. He was recovering from a massive head trauma that resulted from an automobile collision earlier that year. I was both relieved to learn his identity and a little ashamed of my thoughts. I took him to the nearest phone and contacted his parents and brother. I told them he was with me and we made arrangements for them to take custody of him.

My lesson was revealed when the teary-eyed mother thanked me and told me they had been worried sick about him and had prayed he would be all right.

As strange as the circumstances in which you might find yourself, or as distant as our Lord may seem, remember that Jesus knows your heart, and He really is faithful to His people!

> Therefore you do not lack any spiritual gift as you eagerly wait for our Lord Jesus Christ to be revealed. He will keep you strong to the end, so that you will be blameless on the day of our Lord Jesus Christ. God, who has called you into fellowship with his Son Jesus Christ our Lord, is faithful.
> -I Corinthians 1:7-9

I had a lot to do! I was overwhelmed before I ever started the long commute to work. For those of you who don't know me, that would be all the way out to my driveway! It seemed like forever on a day like this. The door slammed behind me and I felt as though I were headed off to my own demise! The boulder on my shoulder was almost more than I could bear. Ever felt that way?

I got into my patrol car, notified the dispatcher I was on duty, and said a little prayer. (Since I was not in school, I thought it would be OK!) I asked God what had happened to all my joy. I was doing this in His service (Romans 13:1-5), so why had He let me down? The songs on my radio say that daily Christian life is supposed to be filled with joy and security. My life seemed filled with only fear and worry.

I said my prayer and headed out to work. I had about an hour before I had to start with all my appointments for the day. I receive numerous complaints about a stretch of highway near my home; I decided to make an appearance. Hopefully people would see me there and ease up on the complaints.

This highway really did need a little enforcement! I started spotting violations and stopping cars. I felt a tinge of hope. Maybe all I needed was to get started. I just *hate* writing tickets. About as much as I *hate* disciplining my kids. I know it is for the drivers' own good, so it makes me feel a little better knowing it's the right thing to do; besides, it's my calling.

As you might know, lots of people complain about how bad everyone drives until they get caught doing something wrong. Yeah, you guessed it. My day wasn't going any better after I started working. I paused, not really in prayer, but I whispered, "What am I doing wrong?" I wondered why it seemed the Lord had abandoned me. Just as I was getting securely perched on my pity pot, I spotted another violator. Not a big deal, but I still felt this driver needed to be stopped.

I was on a two-lane highway with traffic traveling in both directions. As this vehicle approached, I turned on my red lights and motioned for the driver to pull over. It was a female driver in a new vehicle. She didn't pull over very far. As a matter of fact, she stopped right in the middle of the busy highway and this was during rush hour! I pulled my patrol car in behind hers and got out. I heard her yelling something at me as soon as I opened the door.

"Great!" I thought. "Just what I need! I must be being punished for something!" I walked up to the car to visit with this lady about her violation, hoping I would not get run over in the process.

When I arrived at the car, I realized it was my aunt. I dearly love my aunt and have always been especially fond of her because she's a little unpredictable! There I stood in traffic, trying to motion everyone to go around me as I shook my finger at my aunt.

Yeah, I gave her a break. She was really nervous and probably embarrassed at being caught by the person I assume is her favorite nephew! I was trying to get her on her way before someone had an accident trying to go around us, when I felt her hands on my face! She had reached up and was pulling me into the car! In slow motion, I felt my hat hit the car door as my face got pulled in! She puckered up and smooched me like I was ten and at a family reunion!

My first concern was how this looked to everyone going out of his or her way to get around us! They were obviously looking at what the officer was doing, and wondering what was so important that he had to block traffic for it!

A kiss! I know she's my aunt, she knows she's my aunt, but no one else knew it! Fortunately, I have an in-car video camera so I was not too worried about complaints...only rumors!

I walked back to my car trying to sport my humblest pose as I wiped the lipstick off my face and straightened my hat. Needless to say, that was the last stop for the day on that stretch of road! Those of you who live near me can thank my aunt.

As I drove away, I thought about what had just happened. What else was there to do but laugh! I laughed not only at my aunt, but also at my self-pity and at myself. I realized that when I left the house, I was being held captive by my own feelings and emotions. It was not God who had abandoned me for the day. It was my faith.

Our God is always faithful. But we have to make the choice every moment about our faithfulness, about whether or not we are going to stand on our faith or become prisoners because of our lack of it. In the Old Testament, the Lord taught the children of Israel this lesson and made them a promise:

> "The ransomed of the Lord will return. They will enter Zion with singing; everlasting joy will crown their heads. Gladness and joy will overtake them, and sorrow and sighing will flee away."
> -Isaiah 51:11

As it is with all of God's promises, we have to believe in them and then receive or stand on them. Christianity is not a feeling. It is a lifestyle, a lifestyle I am still learning I must choose to live one moment at a time.

CRASH

One of the things I like best about my job is that each day I never know exactly what I will be doing. It is like my own little adventure every day. Each morning I try to pray, asking the Lord to guide my steps and protect my family while I am away. Like most of us, I occasionally forget or get busy right away. I sometimes wonder if there is any correlation to days like the one I relate here and my faithfulness to morning prayers. In any case, when I leave my driveway, I head out into the great "unknown."

I was on the night shift, patrolling the interstate system near my home. It had been a routine night, and my shift was about over so I was in the subliminal shutting-down mode. (Oh, come on! Don't tell me you work diligently until quitting time! All the time?) I was starting to get sleepy when I heard my number called. Great! I shook my head and hoped it was nothing serious enough to warrant staying out past quitting time. I answered the call. It seemed the driver of a red car believed gas was free in Iowa. He helped himself and drove away.

I don't know what it is about gas drive-offs, but I have had bad experiences with them. I knew this time was not good either. I was the only law enforcement officer out for 100 miles of interstate. I don't recall if I remembered to pray at the beginning of my shift, but I distinctly remember doing so when I felt the hair on the back of my neck stand up! I continued driving and looking for this gas thief in his red car. In the dark, all by myself...at times like this I wonder if maybe I missed my calling. Perhaps I was really meant to be wealthy and not work at all.

About the time I started to giggle to myself about my foolish train of thought, I heard that familiar voice come from the pit of my belly. (No, it wasn't my breakfast!) I heard the voice of my constant companion and navigator (Isaiah 30:21) as He pointed the way!

Directly ahead and on the other side of the median! I slowed to cross and see if my gut really knew more than my head. As soon as I got into the grass, I could see the red car take off! (I never should have doubted the location of my brains!)

I got to the other side and caught him rather quickly. I turned on every light on my patrol car to let him know I wanted to "visit" with him for a bit. He was not very welcoming though. He kept going. I told my dispatcher of my location, that I was in a pursuit, and to please find another officer to come and help me. I followed the little red car for about 25 miles before I heard a deputy coming to assist.

Total time: about 13 minutes. You do the math. Once this gas thief finally realized he was not going to out-drive me, he decided to get off the interstate and onto a state highway. It was a bit curvy but I stayed with him, blindly following wherever he led me.

That did not work either, so we started off onto a gravel road. I did not have a clue where I was. I had never been on this road before in my life! But I was determined to follow his taillights wherever they went! They led into a cornfield! Yep, you guessed it! My patrol car and I were in pursuit out in the corn! I consulted my belly: "Where is this guy going?" He must have done something a little worse than steal gas!

I continued to follow in the dark. Deputies from two other counties desperately tried to get to my rapidly-changing location. I could only tell them we were in a field. Big help! I could not see anything but his taillights. My adrenaline was pumping, my belly was now talking in more than one way, and I was determined to talk to this guy. I became fixed on his taillights.

I soon found that my determination blindfolded me. With the best of intentions, my resolve was affecting my judgement.

I followed his lights until they suddenly disappeared! I had a chance to take one breath before I saw no more cornfield! Only a fence, then I felt the crash!

I was right to pursue the thief. I was right to follow him until the end. He was an outlaw, and it is my calling as well as my sworn duty to protect society from his kind of behavior. What was *not* right, however, was for me to become so fixed on his lights that I followed him right over a 20-foot cliff!

 We sometimes do the same in our spiritual lives! With the best of intentions, we trust our own knowledge of scripture. We follow the pastor or the small group leader intently, trusting that God will guide us. We assume that God has put these people in positions of authority and that He has trained and called them into the service of His church. We follow intently, diligently, and faithfully, at times feeling guilty if we question the pastor or teacher.

In the book of Acts, Dr. Luke refers to people like this in chapter 17 verse 10 when he speaks of people whom some may consider to be "falling away" because they don't follow blindly. In this particular passage, the apostle Paul and Silas were traveling to Berea. Luke describes the Bereans as being of "more noble character than the Thessalonians" because "They examine the Scriptures every day to see if what Paul said was true."

Paul, whose letters fill much of the New Testament, was being checked out? And Luke thinks this is a good thing? I pray this is a lesson to us all! Pray for your teachers and your pastor! Follow them intently, diligently, and faithfully. Then check out what they say with the Final Authority: the Bible, the Word of God itself.

[Study] to present yourself to God as one approved, a workman who does not need to be ashamed and who correctly handles the word of truth.
-II Timothy 2:15

SHOPPING TRIP

Gloom enveloped the day and me. I was embarking upon a trip that is undoubtedly one of the more frightening trips a man must endure in life. I was headed to "The Mall" with my wife Tresa. She had money and was determined not to leave the mall until it was all gone. We went from the clothing store to the shoe store and back again as if we were searching for the antidote to some deadly disease.

After the initial fear wore off and I was comfortable with the fact that these women were not going to hurt me during their gathering frenzy, I decided to sit down in one of the chairs provided by the store. These chairs are obviously put there for "The Husband," because they are off in a corner, out of the mainstream of traffic, yet close enough to the dressing rooms to offer a nod of approval.

I took my seat and started observing. I noticed how the female customers interacted with the sales ladies. I found this particular ritual very interesting. Outside in the mall, most of the women walked around almost in a daze, not bothering to even acknowledge the presence of other human life forms. But once they arrived inside the store, their attitude changed to one of almost complete trust in the sales clerks.

I sat in silence as I watched one particular young lady pick out several outfits and rush to the dressing room. (Just for the record, it wasn't Tresa.) She emerged to be intercepted by the sales clerk. They walked over to the mirrors and the young lady faced the clerk, her back to the mirrors. She asked the sales lady some pretty personal questions. She asked this complete stranger how the outfit looked, and if it hid the fat on her thighs. She asked if it would look all right if she lost a few pounds, which she confided had been an ongoing problem. She asked if her husband would find it flattering. She had on a blazer with the skirt, and asked several questions about fashion, like "Could I get away with just a T-shirt under it?" She wondered if this outfit would be O.K. to wear to work. It was most obvious that this young lady was quite concerned about her outward appearance. I found this to be very curious because moments before, I suspect, this young lady would not have even smiled at this clerk who was then playing an active role in her very identity.

As I watched, I decided it must be one of those little attributes unique to females until I witnessed something that just amazed me. After she had finished her questions, the young lady turned toward the mirror to check it out for herself. She was checking in the mirror to see if she agreed with what the sales clerk had said

In this young lady I saw a portrait of us all, men and women alike. We won't go to the store and improve our outward appearance without checking things out for ourselves. We try things on, get an opinion, and look for ourselves to see if we agree with the opinion we have obtained. Or, we look for

ourselves to see if what we have on reflects the image we want to portray.

I learned a valuable lesson about going to church from observing this young lady in the store that day. If we are that concerned about our outward appearance, how much more attention should we pay to our inward appearance? Listen intently to the pastor in church, then check it out for yourself!

> Do your best to present yourself to God as one approved, a workman who does not need to be ashamed and who correctly handles the word of truth.
> -II Timothy 2:15

Little White Line

was assigned to patrol a 46-mile stretch of road, and I was driving around meeting new "friends" and "ministering to them" (see Romans 13:4). The usual heavy traffic sometimes makes it difficult and dangerous to work on this highway. It is hard to turn around, hard to catch up to the people with whom I wish to "visit," and very dangerous to stand on. People say it all the time: "I wouldn't do your job for anything, with all the crazy people out there! You never know what you are going to walk into when you approach a car."

Most people don't realize I am a whole lot more concerned about being run over than I am about being shot at. How many times have you bent down to change the station on the radio and realized you were not where you thought you were on the road when you looked back up? How often have you reached in the back to take care of a child, looked in the glove box, dialed a number on your cell phone, lit a cigarette, or blown your nose while you were driving? Be honest, now! I see it all day long...people driving around not focused on their driving.

It is easy to do. You take care of something other than your driving. You hit the road bumps and hear the noise, then realize you have gotten off track, just a little. It is not a big deal. One we often don't even think about much. In fact, it takes very little effort to correct from the distraction and get back to the appropriate position on the roadway.

You must realize that for a guy like me, that is my biggest fear! A small infraction for you may be a fatal mistake for me! I stand on the side of the road, most of the time very close to or right on that little white line, with 2000-pound missiles traveling directly at me. I do it a dozen times a day and pray every time that the people around me are not complacent about being on "the straight and narrow"!

It had been a pretty routine day. I received a call from my dispatcher about a man riding his bicycle on the interstate! I did not know what I would find. Most of the time, with a call like this, it is a homeless person just trying to get somewhere. That is what I anticipated.

That is not what I found. When I arrived, I found this little guy on a 10-speed bike pulling a kiddy car with a big flag and a map. He was dressed in a helmet and clothes that looked like one of those professional bicyclists. I have worked a huge statewide bike ride long enough to spot someone who is serious about cycling, and this guy fit the bill. When I got a little closer, I noticed a flag sticking out of the top of his helmet. I later found out it was the national flag of Columbia. At the time though, I thought he was just some nutcase with an expensive bicycling outfit!

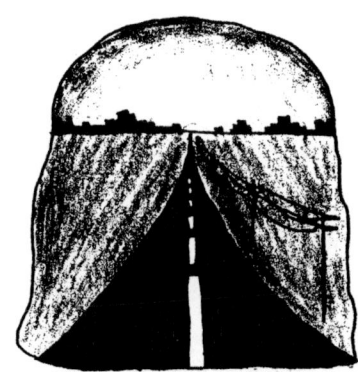 I pulled in behind him and got him to stop. He started digging in his kiddy car. Normally I would put up my guard anticipating some kind of weapon. He just stood there, smiled at me, and waved. He brought his notebook back to my car and handed me his passport. He was born in 1950; he had a wife and several children. He was from Columbia and did not speak very good English. That made it difficult for me to find out what he was doing on the interstate and explain to him how dangerous it was for him to be riding his bike there.

He handed me his notebook with a big grin. I opened it to find business cards from law enforcement officers all over the country! They were stapled in the notebook and had little words of encouragement written beneath them. This was a little odd, so I kept on reading, hoping the comments would reveal what the heck this guy was doing!

I was not the first cop this guy had encountered! Through his broken English and my very bad Spanish, I did get enough out of him to figure out he was riding his bicycle across the country, starting in San Diego and heading to the East Coast. I concluded he was harmless. I gave him a map and traced the route he would need to take to stay off the interstate system and get to the next state. Of course he was not going to get out of my car without a business card, so I gave him one and signed his book. I followed him to the next exit and hoped to get rid of him.

As I followed him, I wondered why someone from Bogota, Columbia would leave his family to ride his bicycle across a country where he couldn't even speak the language! I see a lot of pretty odd things, but my curiosity got the better of me on this one. I chuckled under my breath at this guy peddling just as fast as those little legs could peddle and that Colombian flag waving in the breeze from the top of his helmet.

I looked at the back of the kiddy car which held all of his belongings, including a little baby crib mattress on which he slept. Looking at that, I felt the touch of the Lord's hand on my heart. I knew I had to set aside my cynicism and pay attention because the Lord had a lesson for me here.

It was then I noticed a newspaper article pinned to the back of his cart. Once we got off the interstate, I stopped him again to read the article. A San Diego columnist had written this little guy's story.

The man was here because of what he believed was a call from God. He had a message: he was trying to call attention to the living conditions in his country. He wanted people to know of the poverty of his people and that they need help. He loved the Lord and he cared about his people. He was a faithful man who was trying to make a difference at any cost. He believed the Lord called him to this task, and that was why he was here.

I reached into my pocket and gave him all the cash I had. I sent him on his way. I went back to my car and cried. I thought of what faith and courage this man must have! I cried because I knew that compared to him, I would not measure up. I was ashamed because moments before I had been laughing at him.

This man understood that when the Lord called him to salvation, it was not just an escape hatch from hell but a call to service! He took literally the words in 1 Peter 2:9: "But you are a chosen people, a royal priesthood, a holy nation, a people belonging to God, that you may declare the praises of him who called you out of darkness into his wonderful light."

He did not expect those who had formal training to call attention to his cause. He did not wait for someone who was schooled in fundraising. He did not even wait for someone who knew how to speak the language! He felt the Lord's hand on his heart and he acted! He knew the Lord gave him the right as a believer to declare His praises. He threw out conventional wisdom and trusted in the foolishness of God (I Corinthians 1:18-20).

When he met me, he had peddled his way across half of the continent. There were no TV cameras, no reporters, no one in a van following him in case he broke down. He did not have scheduled checkpoints with a comfortable hotel room waiting where he could rest his aching muscles. Just a little man, in a strange land, where he could barely speak the language, all alone on a bicycle. In spite of all that, he still had the courage to do what he believed the Lord wanted him to do! He did not have the backing of a big church. He was not a professional. He did not even have any money. All he knew was that our God is in control! He must have believed the words from Isaiah:

> "...my word that goes out from my mouth... will not return to me empty, but will accomplish what I desire and achieve the purpose for which I sent it."
> -Isaiah 55:1

As you think of what you would like to accomplish in this next year, please don't forget to consider what plans the Lord has made for you. Please don't make the mistake of getting distracted, even for a moment, from the cause to which we are all called (Mark 16:15-20). It may seem like a little distraction, like the one while you are driving and reach to quickly change the radio station. But don't forget that for someone, it may be an eternally fatal mistake.

The next time the Lord gives you the opportunity to share His love, even if you think it is too risky, remember me standing on the side of the road, on that little white line. Think of where you are on the "straight and narrow," then be inspired by the courage and faith of my new friend Obando Ramirez.

MARKED MAN

Responsibilities and the uniform make me a marked man. When I enter a restaurant, someone usually points to a companion and calls out to me, "Here he is! He's the one you've been looking for!"

When parents direct a child's attention to me and threaten the child with "You behave or he will take you away," I take time to correct the parent in front of the child.

When you're late and racing down the road, whose marked car is it you look for?

And as you drive along and spot me and my patrol car, whom do you watch once you've tapped your brakes? Whose actions do you check out? Who feels like a caged monkey in a public zoo?

Even when I go into the grocery store of my small hometown, I get quizzed about the "inside scoop" on the latest crime news.

Because I work on an interstate system, I encounter travelers from various parts of the country. However, they all share four characteristics when the weather gets bad:

1. They expect me to know exactly what the weather is like wherever they are headed.

2. They expect me to know the road conditions at any given place in the continental United States.

3. They expect me to tell them which roads to take.

4. They expect me to predict their future and tell them if they will arrive at their destination safely.

A now-retired former partner practiced a winter weather ritual whenever we stopped for dinner. He would lay on the edge of our table a napkin on which he had written these words: "The roads stink. Don't ask." People would walk over, pause to read the napkin, and then ask anyway. Because it was our duty, one of us would answer in a friendly voice and try to be helpful. Secretly, we wondered how that person would respond if *we* interrupted *his* dinner break to ask a question whose answer was beyond the realm of any human knowledge.

After dinner on a typical Iowa winter weather day, I got up to use the restroom and left my dinner partners at the table to answer travel questions. I chatted briefly with a man on his way out, and then noticed that the stall was empty. I could sit there and enjoy a moment of peace and anonymity. Finally, I was all alone for just a few moments.

I thought of my friends at the dinner table struggling to finish their meals while being bombarded with travelers. For just a split second I lamented, then decided to stay put for just a little longer. The restroom door opened. Someone walked in. Only silence followed. "He wouldn't dare!" I thought.

I realized he had spotted the bottom of my uniform pants and my shiny shoes as he tapped on the stall door. "Excuse me," came the voice, "but can you tell me what the roads are like?"

I was dumbfounded that anyone would ask me a question assuming the position I must be in.

"Sir," I replied, "I'm afraid not. I really can't see any road conditions from here."

He got the hint. He turned around and left quietly.

This story has another point: weary travelers wander about all the time. They travel through life without much direction, unsure of what lies ahead, uncertain of which road to take. Some have been caught in a storm or two and are afraid. Some have experienced pain and suffering. Some have been involved in fender benders; others have endured lasting damage. We can't know what lies ahead on their spiritual journeys, but we can direct them to the One with the "inside scoop," the One who has given us a road map that routes us through all of life's storms.

In II Corinthians 1:21-22, Paul assured us, "Now it is God who makes both us and you stand firm in Christ. He anointed us, set his seal of ownership on us, and put his Spirit on our hearts as a deposit, guaranteeing what is to come."

While my uniform makes me a "marked man," we are all marked as we wear the "badge" of almighty God pinned on our hearts and as we are armed with the sword of the spirit. The responsibility of our great commission also marks us, for many will perish on the stormy roads of life unless we point them in the right direction. We can't just sit in the stall and hope they will simply go away or trust that someone else will provide directions!

Romans 1:16a provides the "how" and "why" of being "marked men." It encourages us:

> For I am not ashamed of the gospel, because it is the power of God for the salvation of everyone who believes.

A New Beginning

Most of my life, I have wanted to follow God, but I have been unsure of what it is I am supposed to do. I hope I am not alone in this uncertainty. I believe a fine line separates our plans and visions and what "the master outline" says. As I look back, I remember countless little adventures I have embarked upon fully believing it was the Lord's will that I experience them, full of visions and what each would be like.

When I was 17, a man came up to me and told me about a new job that would lead me on a life-long "adventure." I was to be trained, clothed, and fed. It was not like any other job because this was going to be "fun." The kick to it all was that I was to be paid and given money for a college education. I could not wait until I turned 18 and could start the rest of my life!

Since I believed I already knew everything, it was about time I spread my wings to fly! And what a break, to run into an opportunity like this so young in life! I was certain the Lord's hand was involved! It had to be. All of my friends were making arrangements for loans and applying for scholarships while I landed a cushy deal like this one! I sent up prayers of thanksgiving time after time while I waited anxiously to start my new "job." The day finally came, and I boarded the plane for the West Coast! Off to California just like the "Beverly Hillbillies"!

The mental picture I had painted of my new adventure was not quite what I found when I stepped off of the bus at the Marine Corps Recruit Training Facility, affectionately referred to as "the depot."

As I arrived, a welcoming committee greeted me. The first members of this committee to whom I was introduced were Marine Corps drill instructors. They boarded the bus to greet us and welcome us to the depot in their own special way. I had never been greeted quite like this before! They must have been having a really bad day because they did not seem very happy. They yelled and screamed all kinds of things that would be inappropriate to repeat.

I had been 18 years old for about one whole month as I got off that bus to stand on a set of yellow footprints painted on the pavement at the depot. The footprints were in the correct position of a platoon formation with each set at the position of attention. It was my introduction to the next three months of my life. Nothing I had done prior to this moment was acceptable in the eyes of those appointed to "remold" me. They would teach me a new way to walk, talk, dress, eat, sleep, go to the restroom (yes, nothing was sacred!), shower, even just stand around.

I was soon introduced to the next members of the welcoming committee, the barbers. Just for the record, as I sat down in the chair, they did not ask me how I wanted it cut. After we were all trimmed and dressed in a new set of clothes, we packed away all our civilian gear into a box that would not be seen again until we earned the title of Marine. These items were the final reminders of the life we were leaving behind.

I went through the next three days virtually without any sleep. The drill instructors took turns keeping us up, yelling at us mostly. Because whatever we did was not right, we did it over and over. I thought a lot about what I was doing there, as

I'm sure everyone else did. I have never been so scared in all of my life. I was thrown into a completely foreign environment. I was dressed in clothes that in high school were not at all "cool." I had a haircut that prevented me from putting on T-shirts without needing to run a lint brush over my head. I was yelled at constantly by people I had never met before.

I prayed about this decision before I signed my life away to these people. I really believed this is where the Lord led me. I asked God many times why He had sent me there. I can testify whole-heartedly that this was not part of *my* vision!

As I look back, I am reminded of Proverbs 16:9: "In his heart a man plans his course, but the Lord determines his steps." I remember constantly asking God what I had just "stepped in" because from where I stood, it did not smell very good.

I quickly learned that surviving in this new environment meant I would have to become something I was not: A new me. Many times it was a new me that I did not want to become.

I struggled with the life I once had. It was the little things I missed the most. Like not having to ask permission to speak. Having to ask permission to "make a head call" (go to the restroom) was really a chore. I remember my early learning experience. First, I had to ask for permission to speak. Once that was granted, I requested permission to make a head call. The drill instructed said "No." OK, what do I do now? I had to go! I dreaded this anyway so I had waited as long as I possibly could. Tough decisions have to be made, so at the top of my lungs I yelled, "Sir, this recruit requests permission to make an emergency head call." This apparently worked because I was given permission. Thank the Lord! I started to race for the head and got about two steps when I heard a loud "Stop freak!" I began to panic. What now?

"You said there was an emergency but I don't see any sirens!" My head sank; my bladder was pulsing. I raised my hand to the top of my head, opening and closing my fist.

"That's better!" I heard. Finally, I thought! I took off again and got four steps this time before I heard him again. "I see a siren but I don't hear anything." With my palm flexing above my head, I made a siren noise at the top of my lungs as I raced around the formation of my fellow recruits. Into the head I went. To continue the humiliation, I was required to keep it up until the emergency was over.

This was not at all what I thought it would be like. It was certainly not like anything I had ever experienced in my life or ever dreamed of, for that matter. I felt completely blind! Each new moment brought new light to what I was becoming. My eyes opened to a new world that was completely foreign to me.

Our Christian walk is the same way. " 'I will lead the blind by ways they have not known, along unfamiliar paths I will guide them; I will turn the darkness into light before them and make the rough places smooth. These are the things I will do; I will not forsake them,' " promises God in Isaiah 42:16.

Sometimes, gloom clouds our lives. Isaiah did not say that we will stumble blindly down these dark paths and the Lord will rescue us when we get there. Rather, he wrote that the Lord will lead us down these paths. He will put us in situations that may seem hopeless; sometimes, He will put us in places that make us question what the heck we are doing here, just as I did at boot camp. It has been my personal experience that when we are in such a situation, we run out of our own answers before we finally remember to ask for the Lord's guidance and help. I admit that I do so only after I have exhausted all other possible choices.

Consider it pure joy, my brothers, when you face trials of many kinds, because you know that the testing of your faith develops perseverance. Perseverance must finish its work so that you may be mature and complete, not lacking anything.

-James 1:2-4

THE HARVEST

or nearly 32 years, my father has been in the law enforcement profession. During the time I have been in law enforcement, he has been a constant source of wisdom. One of the most valuable pieces of advice he has shared with me is this: "Watch the guy who is watching you."

That is exactly what happened this day. I was on routine patrol when I met a blue car with no front license plate - a relatively small offense. It was the driver and passengers that really caught my attention. They stared at me like I was riding naked on horseback through a revival tent meeting! I remembered what my father had said, so I found a place to turn around so I could go "visit" with them!

I could tell right away that they were not anxious to meet me. They sped away, weaving in and out of traffic. That was my first clue that there was more to their curious staring at me than my good looks!

I knew right away this was going to turn into a pursuit. The adrenaline flowed, the muscles in my neck and back tensed, and my heart pounded. This was far from my first pursuit, but there is always that suspicion, "Why are they running?" In my mind, they had done little wrong. They must be more afraid of meeting me than facing the consequences of their minor traffic offense. That alone is enough to make me a little nervous.

Every time I walk out the door, just for a fleeting second, I wonder, "Is this the last time I will leave here?" I push it out of my mind, thinking it's a little too morbid, maybe even taboo to think it.

"Will I make it home from work tonight?" If I am to be honest, I think it, then quickly put it out of my mind and kiss my wife and children.

These particular bad guys quickly learned that they were not going to out-drive me on the highway, so they took their chances on the gravel. Up and down, through winding county roads. They were running from me for a reason. When I got close enough to check the license plate on the car, I found out why. The car was stolen! (Thanks for the advice, Dad…I think!)

I tried desperately to find another officer to come to my aid. There were three of them in the car that I could see, and only one of me. The closest trooper was over 50 miles away and the only county deputy was busy doing something else. Finally, a city officer in a small town about 20 miles away left the city limits and headed in my direction! I tried to direct him to where we were going, but every time I thought I had it figured out, they changed course me! It was starting to look like it was going to be just them and me!

Things took a turn for the worse when they left the gravel road and tried their luck in a farm field! I had no choice but to follow them. I could see the front-seat passenger reaching under the seat for something as we headed off the road into the field. I was trying to keep the city officer informed about where I was and what was going on, so as I told him we had left the road, I also told him about the movements of the passenger.

As we headed out into the field, I could see that it was very hilly. The other officer would not be able to see me from the road. I tried to think ahead and deal with the "what ifs" before they happened so I would be prepared. What if they are leading me back into this field where no one can see me so they can start shooting at me? I could see them reaching for something. I turned on my siren and left it on. I told the officer to listen for my siren to locate me. He wouldn't be able to see me because of the hills and the valley they had led me into, but if he would listen, he would be able to hear.

As we traveled through the field, I soon encountered an obstacle: a fence. I could see them on the other side driving up a hill and out of the valley. I deliberately looked around to see where they crossed over. Just for a brief moment I hesitated, looking for a gate. I decided if I did not take some drastic action, they were going to get away!

I decided to ram the fence! I took it out with the front end of my patrol car and a little help from the windshield and the top light bar! I continued the pursuit. I soon found myself back on the road...by myself! They were no where to be found! I had lost them.

About a month later, I learned they were picked up in a neighboring state. When they broke down, a trooper stopped to help them, discovered their crime, and brought them to justice.

My father's good advice applies to us as Christians. When people learn that you are a believer, they will be watching. Will they be watching because they are running from something themselves? It is not just police officers who have to deal with the fact that any day might be their last. Each and every one of us faces the same unexpected possibility of the end of our lives - regardless of our professions!

What about those who watch you because they know you are a Christian? If today were their last day, would they be ready? How about you?

I encourage you to listen for the sound of God's voice. Is He calling you to "chase" someone? Is He calling you to drive down into a valley and turn on your siren for all to hear?

I hesitated, and the people I was chasing got away. Know that just like the people I was after, *everyone* will be brought to justice some day (Romans 14:11). It is my prayer that you learn from my mistake.

Don't hesitate!

Take every opportunity the Lord provides to share the love of Jesus! It may be your last opportunity!

> Then he said to his disciples, "The harvest is plentiful but the workers are few."
> -Matthew 9:37

BABY BEAR

Hidden insecurity lies buried within all of us. It is a collection of little fears that sometimes surface like a ghost and strike at us from within - as happened to me one particular night. Pride keeps it forever etched in my memory.

As a new trooper, I hadn't been patrolling alone for very long. I was working on the interstate system when I received a call from the dispatcher to investigate an accident on one of the off-ramps. The call seemed routine and I wasn't worked up about it.

Arriving at the accident location, I found a bobtail semi (no trailer attached) sitting by itself. As I got closer, the driver rushed toward my patrol car. I couldn't see much damage to his vehicle and no one had reported any injuries, bu he was clearly very excited about something.

Then the "magic" began.

Those in law enforcement know too well about the "magic," a moment some officers crave like a drug while others fear it as they lie awake at night. Contrary to "top cop" shows and "real police video" programs, most of my life as an officer is routine. I answer routine calls and deal with routine problems day in and day out. But there comes a moment when things are transformed, when the routine becomes something unexpected, something new, and that moment is when the excitement begins, when the "magic" happens. Adrenaline surges; the heart pounds; hair bristles on the back of the neck.

With each year I spend in service, I experience the "magic" less often. But that night as I saw the semi driver rush toward my patrol car, I felt the "magic." Before he spoke a word, I knew this was not a routine call.

He explained that a pickup had run into the front of his truck as he exited the interstate system. After the crash, the pickup driver proceeded to get onto the interstate and head west, in the *eastbound* lane!

This was well before everyone had cell phones and could swamp us with reports of the errant driver's whereabouts. All I could do at that time was pick up my radio and notify the dispatcher of the problem.

After telling the semi driver to stay put, I sped away with my red lights on, fully expecting to catch up with the pickup in a matter of minutes. Over my CB (citizens' band) radio, I called for help from anyone nearby. I got instant responses from others who had narrowly missed the pickup traveling the wrong way. I was headed east trying to catch him as I notified my dispatcher over a different radio of my efforts. Other officers were heading in my direction, but as usual, they were all quite far away.

A few people had stopped and phoned in 911 reports to my dispatcher. The pickup driver was no longer headed the wrong way and could be easily spotted: his right front tire was flattened in the collision with the semi and he was now driving on only a rim and throwing sparks everywhere. I would have to hurry to catch up with him.

Soon I was notified he had exited the interstate and was heading toward a large city. I radioed ahead to request assistance from the city officers.

The "magic" of the hunt continued, and as new trooper, I was enjoying every minute of it. I had visions of grandeur as I imagined myself capturing this flagrant lawbreaker. I alone would keep society safe from harm tonight when I rid it of this dangerous criminal!

The city officers soon notified me they had the pickup stopped just south of town on the highway. Three officers were waiting for me to arrive. They reported the driver had a broken clavicle, was in a great deal of pain, and was drunk.

The "magic" turned to fear. I began to panic. I had never arrested a drunk driver by myself. Training officers had always been there to help before. This time, three seasoned city officers would be present and watching *me* arrest this driver!

Fear struck at the heart of my insecurity. I was a rookie. But I didn't want to be known and laughed at by my peers because of it. I arrived and put on my best "seasoned cop" face and tried hard not to make a fool of myself.

Everything went well, and I realized I had not given my fellow officers enough credit. My baby face alone surely gave away my lack of experience. But these three officers offered their assistance only when they could sense I was a little uncertain about what to do in the whole process. I soon realized I was not to be made fun of, but rather encouraged in my inexperience by these three veterans. They offered to take me  under their wings and show me "the ropes" in their city. As a result, I learned that being turned loose on my own did not mean I knew everything, but it was my license to continue learning without the support of my training officers.

As Christians, we feel the same way at times. We think that because we are believers, we should "act" a certain way. And we should, but not to the extent that we pretend to be someone or something we are not. Jesus Himself said, "My grace is sufficient for you, for my power is made perfect in weakness" (II Corinthians 12:9a).

The grace of our Lord is more than enough to cover all our weaknesses, failures, insecurities, and wash them away. That is the real magic! Through God's grace, we are transformed. The old "routine" self becomes something unexpected, something new. The excitement begins, and the real "magic" happens.

The next time we are tempted to "act" Christian, we would do well to remember the Lord might be trying to use our shortcomings! We can be ourselves, be genuine, be real. That is the freeing transforming power of God!

...for all have sinned and fall short of the glory of God, and are justified freely by his grace through the redemption that came by Christ Jesus.
                    - Romans 3:23-24

THIS OLD HOUSE

A certain level of self-confidence is vital if a law enforcement officer is to perform his/her related duties every day. Self-confidence walks a fine line with the male ego, which my wife says is one of my best qualities! And as a Christian male, that fine line is a border that must be heavily guarded. Anyway we look at it, sin is sin! And once we allow sin into our lives, we open the door for some very ungodly results.

If we're honest, it's not macho to be submissive to the Lord. All that talk about being submissive and a servant just isn't appealing to the male ego. Not to mention all that talk about the marriage supper of the lamb when Christ will take His "bride." Thinking of myself as a bride does absolutely nothing to enhance my masculine side! The dangerous aspect of such thoughts is that we also assume a worldly view of faith that insists trusting in something that cannot be seen is but a crutch for the weak.

One winter evening, I was driving around the countryside on patrol. There was little to no traffic: everyone else was at home.

New snowflakes refracted the moonlight, making the rural countryside glisten like heaven. The night should have been captured in a glass ball.

I basked in the solitude. Even the county deputy, usually the only officer I can count on for help, was out of the area on a trip.

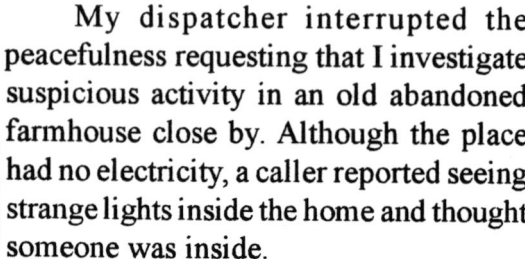 My dispatcher interrupted the peacefulness requesting that I investigate suspicious activity in an old abandoned farmhouse close by. Although the place had no electricity, a caller reported seeing strange lights inside the home and thought someone was inside.

I found the "Amityville Horror" house right in the middle of the Iowa countryside! No yard light illuminated the ancient house, which had obviously been abandoned a long time ago. It was surrounded by winter remnants of overgrown bushes. I found fresh footprints in the snow! No problem! I don't believe in the "boogie man."

But then again, it could be some wandering vagrant lunatic or maybe a drug lab. This solitude wasn't all I had it cracked up to be! No help was available in a 50-mile area.

I approached the house slowly, addressing the question of believing in unseen things and flirting with the ego issue. "Just exactly how macho do I want to be right now?...Do I submit to our Savior and hope He has a little of that salvation for this situation?...Or do I approach as if I see nothing but a possibility?"

There was certainly no campfire in the living room. Just a few footprints, a remote chance there might be something in there. "Well, it can't be proven either way until I take a look. After all, seeing is believing, right?" I chose to remain cautious since I was all alone. I neared the house and checked the door. Why it was locked was beyond me. Just my luck, though.

I sort of ducked under one of the many broken windows. ("Sort of ducked" because while getting injured in the line of duty may be necessary, getting dirty in the line of duty is out of the question!) I quickly looked in the window and saw nothing. I carefully climbed in, brushed myself off, and took a look around. The house seemed vacant with no signs of anyone having been there for quite some time. I continued to check the other rooms, almost embarrassed by some of the silly thoughts I'd had driving up. Just another routine trip. No drug dealers, no vagrants, no lunatics, no boogie men! Just an old house. More than likely, a spooked housewife alone in the middle of nowhere had made the report.

I continued checking the rest of the house, shining my flashlight into the rooms and quickly throwing shadows about, when I briefly glimpsed a man standing in a doorway!

Forget about getting dirty! I quickly dropped to the floor and rolled against the wall. Dead silence. I tried hard to listen for the sound of any movement while my bladder tried desperately to hold back that last cup of coffee. The only thing moving was my heart causing dust from the floor to dance across my freshly pressed uniform!

I crawled to the doorway, then reached for my flashlight to illuminate the room before I stuck my head through the doorway. Still no movement. I took a quick peek into the room and there he was: an old paint sheet thrown over a closet door!

> So we fix our eyes not on what is seen, but on what is unseen. For what is seen is temporary, but what is unseen is eternal.
> -II Corinthians 4:18

Home Alone

I was awakened from a sound sleep by a crash! I heard voices and sounds of a tank rolling through my living room! What could it be? A severe storm? A tornado? I sprang from my bed, wiped the sleep from my eyes, and rushed to the window. Adrenaline surged through my veins as I thought of my family and their safety. I drew open the blind to be greeted by the sun. I was thankful the noise I heard was not a violent storm, but something was going on downstairs! Still half asleep, I cautiously walked down the stairs to do battle with this army of intruders. The sound grew louder with every step. As the last stair squeaked, I rounded the corner to face my adversary. I focused my eyes as my heart pounded in my chest. There they were.

My children! It was Monday, and my wife Tresa had left for a two-week school. She left me with the kids - home alone.

My children were all pretty young then. I had taken time off from work to cover the household responsibilities. The apostle Paul instructed me to "lay down my life" for my wife (Ephesians 5:25). Unknowingly, I discovered that is precisely what I had agreed to do! The struggles were great and the trials were many, but I figured with the Lord on my side, how hard could it be?

Well, standing before me were my "little blessings," and I had to figure out what to do now. My mom always said, "Breakfast is the most important meal of the day," so I figured that would be a good place to start. Into the kitchen we went for a well-balanced, gourmet bowl of Trix for everyone! I was done in about ten minutes, refreshed and ready to start the day. The kids, however, saw fit to spend about 45 minutes eating. I realized my children did not understand the concept of having a "mission." Or have any interest what-so-ever in accomplishing it.

Thankfully that 45 minutes gave me some additional time to fine-tune my plan of attack (kids, dishes, clothing, etc.), and do some close-range recon work (laundry pile, toys on the floor, etc.). I sized up my mission objectives as I watched my children decorate their pajamas with the milk and cereal. Never in my wildest dreams would I have imagined three little children could eat so slowly and get into something so rapidly after they were finished!

As the day progressed, I felt a surge of enlightenment. Trying to imagine the time span of eternity didn't seem all that difficult to me now. I knew it had to be very close to the segment of time between sunrise and naptime.

And naptime finally did arrive…a time for Dad to catch a breath of fresh air and recuperate. I tried to catch up on all the things I was prevented from doing with the kids around. I was tired, and it was only about noon on the first day!

I heard the couch and remote control calling me with all of the lustful wooing of a beautiful enchantress! I knew I had to be strong and "avoid the temptation." The kitchen was a good starting place, so back to the scene of the initial crime I went.

As a police officer I have seen many accidents. I have seen bodies twisted and mangled. I have seen tragedy and ruined lives, at times on a monumental scale. In short, I have been forced to witness sights that would make some toss and turn in a cold sweat during the night. So I asked myself, "Why Lord? Why does the thought of cleaning out the kitchen sink strainer make my stomach heave?"

Feeling the need for some divine intervention, I looked toward heaven for strength. My answer came. I found a new "copyist" error in my Bible. In Genesis 2:18 where God created Eve, instead of reading "and the Lord God said it is not good for man to be alone," it should read "and the Lord God said *man cannot handle being alone.*"

I learned a very valuable lesson in those two weeks.

Some of the things we take for granted in our daily lives are really treasures sent from heaven. God placed them right under our noses. It is a shame we often don't realize the many blessings the Lord has given us until they are gone.

Thankfully mine came back!

I write this story in praise of my beautiful wife. These verses from Proverbs describe her best:

A wife of noble character who can find?
She is worth far more than rubies.
Her husband has full confidence in her...
-Proverbs 31:10-11

Many women do noble things, but you
surpass them all. Charm is deceptive,
and beauty is fleeting; but a woman who
fears the Lord is to be praised.
Give her the reward she has earned, and
let her works bring her praise at
the city gate.
                    -Proverbs 31:29-31

Husbands, take time to be thankful for your wife.

Then take time to tell her.

SHOTS FIRED

This story is one I thought I would never put down on paper because I could see no lessons evolve from it. This event is one I will not forget as long as I live.

I had been a police officer for three years, and in my current assignment for less than three months. In short, I still knew it all. But little did I know before I went to work this night, the Lord would show me things that would be the source of many questions which haunt me to this day.

I was assigned to patrol a 100-mile stretch of road in the western half of the state. I was just finishing my field training and still riding with one of my training officers. I was driving along trying to show my training officer that I had things under control when we heard a broadcast on the police radio.

The dispatcher reported a theft of gasoline from a truck stop close to our location. The thief was driving a little blue car with the back window broken out. Even in the dark, that should not be too hard to find. We called another officer in our same area and planned that he would sit in the median watching for the little blue car while we kept traveling west until one of us intercepted the vehicle.

No problem! This would be a relatively easy assignment. I kept driving with my eyes open for this little blue car, pretending to be alert. After all, I had to let my training officer know I was ready to "fly solo." And it was the middle of the night!

After a few minutes, we heard that the other officer had the vehicle in sight only a few miles ahead of us and was about to stop the driver. So much for that call, I thought.

Suddenly, a very excited voice came on the radio. "Shots fired! I need an ambulance!"

My heart jumped and the hair on the back of my neck stood straight up. I was cold. An eerie mood drifted into the car; it was like slipping into another dimension on the "Twilight Zone."

I looked at my training officer in the passenger seat. His eyes were as big as mine. I pushed the accelerator to the floor. We did not know who had been shot, who was doing the shooting, or who needed the ambulance. Fear raced through my body as I considered what we might find once we arrived. Terror set in when I considered what I might encounter once we got there.

I was traveling as fast as the car would go. Cars drifted by the passenger side as if they were traveling in slow motion. Even a rocket scientist like myself could figure out something pretty heavy was going down. I needed help. Instinctively, my training was taking control. My mind filled with all the things I had been taught in preparation for a moment like this. My stomach fluttered with butterflies that found their way in.

Thankfully, I could also feel the Lord's hand on my heart. I did not know what I would encounter, but I knew the Lord was going with me. My mind flooded with a lot of thoughts, one of which was, "Thank you Lord! I am so thankful you are coming along on this one. Just please don't take me with you when you go!"

Soon I saw lights from the other patrol car. We pulled in behind it and found the officer standing near the front. Just standing there. He didn't have his gun out. No shootout in progress. No bodies lying on the pavement. Just the other officer standing there, clutching his first aid kit.

We exited our patrol car and raced up to greet him, thankful he was all right. As I approached him, I could tell something was deathly wrong. He was white as a ghost! As we got closer, he said, "You guys are going to have to take care of this. I am not going back up there." He motioned toward the little blue car. After a little small talk about what had happened, I approached the car.

I saw the broken glass in the back seat. As my flashlight panned the interior of the car, I saw the blood. In the backseat, behind the driver's seat, I saw a small black-haired, eight-year-old little boy, laying face up. He wore a little league football T-shirt. His head rested on a football like a pillow. His eyes were open. The left side of his head was missing. It was a bullet wound, caused by a 38-caliber revolver.

I continued to move my flashlight around the inside of the car. I followed the backseat over to the passenger side. I stopped once again in absolute horror when I saw the backside of a little girl. She was four years old. She was slumped over behind the passenger seat facing the floor.

I later learned from one of the investigating officers that she watched her big brother get shot in the side of the head by their mother, the driver. She pleaded, "Please don't shoot me, Mommy!" as the woman fired one round through the back window, breaking the glass. The little girl jumped around in the backseat in an attempt to avoid getting shot when another round was fired at her. This one lodged in the headliner of the car. One more round was fired. This one hit her in the forehead. She died in the backseat, next to her big brother.

Mom continued to drive until the officer assisting us stopped her. When he approached the car, she simply told him, "My kids are dead. The gun is still in the car." When I arrived, she was sitting in the front seat of the patrol car in handcuffs.

I was in shock. When I heard the Lord's call to the ministry of law enforcement (Romans 13:1-4), this is not what I had in mind. I did not know what to do. I simply asked God "WHY?" He still has not answered me.

I have seen a lot of death in my career. Unfortunately, this was not the last time I would have to deal with the death of children. But hopefully, this was the last time I will see children killed by their mother. I pray I never have to deal with such a heinous crime ever again.

I can recall the face of this woman who murdered her innocent little children. I see their faces. The anger wells up inside me again.

I hear the Lord say, "Why are *you* angry? *I died for that woman.*" I know better, but I want to believe that the Lord died only for the good people in the world who had "little" sins.

I sit here writing this in tears. It is so far beyond my comprehension that the Lord would hang on the cross and die for the likes of her. But I know He did. I don't know if this woman has come to a saving knowledge of our Lord Jesus. I do know that if she would ask, He would forgive her.

Scripture states, "If we confess our sins, he is faithful and just and will forgive our sins and purify us from all unrighteousness" (1 John 1:9). Notice the verse does not say anything about putting sin into different categories. Sin is sin.

Our God is so awesome, He would not only forgive her and let her into His flock, but also He would take this terrible sin and remove it "as far as the east is from the west" (Psalm 103:12).

Jesus Himself said,

> "For God so loved the world, that he gave his one and only Son, that whoever believes in him shall not perish but have eternal life. For God did not send his Son into the world to condemn the world, but to save the world through him."
> -John 3:16-17

If our God is willing to forgive the mother who murdered her children, how willing should we be to forgive each other for our petty little differences?

How willing should we be to forgive ourselves?

How willing and open should we be to accept His forgiveness for us?

Don't wait.

Do it now!

Among Us

D uring the years I spent serving as an accident reconstructionist, I was witness to more death and tragedy than I care to think about. Lives lost, broken and shattered, all in the blink of an eye. I am the one left to clean up the mess, to determine exactly how and why things happened the way they did.

The lives of the surviving loved ones were forever changed. They looked to me for answers. They often wanted just to know "why." I would go through the collisions over and over in my head. I would see the evidence again and again. I would see the faces in my sleep. I found that most often I would be looking for the same answer.

WHY?

I could go on endlessly about different collisions I have covered and some of the answers that have dropped from heaven, but this particular story wasn't even one of my cases. I helped a friend with it. It will stand out in my memory till the day I go home. It speaks for itself.

I have covered countless collisions of this kind. Two vehicles traveling in opposite directions meet toward the center of a gravel road, in the country, in the middle of nowhere. This collision was no different. One vehicle contained a single male driver. A young man and his five-year-old son occupied the other vehicle. There were no witnesses. The single male occupant was killed on impact. In the other vehicle were a young man, broken and bloody, and a very frightened little boy.

I can only imagine the thoughts that were going through this little boy's mind. He had just been in a serious automobile collision. Dad is hurt very badly. The sun was about to set. He is in unfamiliar territory. Not a single house was within sight. Regardless of the fear that had to be in his heart, this little boy picked a direction and started running for help. He guessed correctly, and the direction he chose was towards the closest farmhouse.

He got help, but it was too late for Daddy. As the sun set over the horizon, his daddy's life went with it.

The community's heart went out to this little boy. Because of his brave little heart, they nominated him for a hero award. People from the local newspaper went out to his home to ask him questions for an article. They talked about a lot of things. One of the questions they asked was, "How did you decide which direction to run for help?"

I see the face of my own son looking up with eyes that reveal an innocent heart not yet corrupted by a world of lies and deception.

The five-year-old looked at the reporters with that "you guys are silly" look in his eyes.

Then he answered. "That nice lady in the white dress took me there."

My World

Serving as an accident investigator, I see the results of many collisions, some worse than others. When two objects traveling in different paths collide, the world changes for all those involved. There was a time when, through my eyes, heaven and earth collided. My world was changed, forever.

February 1, 1980, I turned 12 years old. I had a party planned with a few of my friends invited to come over to the house. It was my special day. My parents, my brother, my family and friends would all come over and shower me with gifts. My brother David was going to stay home sick from school. We had a long talk the night before, and he told me he really didn't feel all that bad, he just didn't feel much like going. I teased him about playing "hooky" and left.

I was excited as I went to school. I didn't do very much and I had a hard time paying attention in class. Despite my lack of attention to the lessons being taught, by the end of the day, I would be overwhelmed with the things I was to learn.

I was in math class when the phone on the classroom wall rang. It was the principal's office. The teacher conversed for a while on the phone, then informed me I was to gather my things and go to the principal's office. My friends teased me and joked that my parents were giving me time off from school because it was my birthday. It sounded good to me, so I gathered my things and hurried down to the office. I was very happy to get out of school early. What a truly special day this would be! An early start on my presents! So I thought.

As I rounded the corner to the office, I found my uncle standing in the hallway. That would be lesson number one in body language. Even though my uncle was a seasoned veteran of a large metro police department and very good at hiding emotion under pressure, I could tell by the look on his face that I was not on my way to a surprise birthday party. I asked him what was going on. He just grabbed my hand and said, "Your brother is in the hospital."

He led me out to his car and we started the trip downtown. The trip, as I remember, was a pretty quiet one. After a while I asked him what was the matter with David. He simply said that it was similar to the problem he had in the past.

Next to the hospital stood a Methodist church with a big green cross on top. In silence, I looked up and the cross became visible. As my eyes focused on the cross, I felt the Lord's hand on my heart. I could almost feel His presence completely surround me. I then knew that my big brother had died.

I remember getting off the elevator and seeing my aunts and uncles in the hallway next to a display case of dolls dressed in nursing clothes. They were all crying and had a look of sympathy on their faces as my uncle led me into a small room where my parents, my pastor, and my grandma were sitting. I sat down between my mom and dad as the pastor proceeded to tell me that David had gone on to be with the Lord. I will never forget the look on my mother's and father's faces as I looked up at them. I was looking for a signal. I was confused and I wanted to know what I was supposed to do. I already knew that my brother was gone. The Lord had already told me. I wanted to know how I was supposed to react. I felt the Lord's arms wrapped around me so tightly that I was numb. I didn't feel much like crying. Some would say I was in shock, or I was too young to fathom the events that had taken place.

I would argue. I was too young to "cast this care upon the Lord" (1 Peter 5:7). He knew that and in His mercy took it from me, for a time.

At that moment I did cry, but not for my brother. I cried because I could see the pain on my mom's and dad's faces. For me, Heaven and Earth collided that day. One minute it was hello, the next it was good-bye. In this new world I found that I had changed, swallowed up by what remained.

It will happen again, to us all. I pray that we are all prepared...

Brothers, we do not want you to be ignorant about those who fall asleep, or to grieve like the rest of men, who have no hope. We believe that Jesus died and rose again and so we believe that God will bring with Jesus those who have fallen asleep in him. According to the Lord's own word, we tell you that we who are still alive, who are left till the coming of the Lord, will certainly not precede those that have fallen asleep. For the Lord himself will come down from heaven, with a loud command, with the voice of the archangel and with the trumpet call of God, and the dead in Christ will rise first. After that, we who are still alive and are left will be caught up together with them in the clouds to meet the Lord in the air. And so we will be with the Lord forever.
                                    -I Thessalonians 4:13-17

T he stories in this book are very dear to my heart. They are the reflection of the Lord I see when I pray to my God, my personal savior. I have my own relationship with Him. It is personal, and at times very private. I have shared some of the lessons He has taught me with the hope that you would grow closer to Him and nurture your relationship with the Almighty.

It is also my prayer that if some of the words in these pages seem foreign to you, if maybe you do not quite understand what I am talking about when it comes to knowing God in a personal way, then you will rethink where you stand in life.

Life is very precious and tremendously fragile. It can be taken away quickly. Because I am unfortunate enough to witness this frequently, I pray you will take a moment and consider your own humanity.

God's word talks of our humanity in Romans 3:23: "...for all have sinned and fallen short of the glory of God..."

We are all sinners. Because of the fall of Adam, we are born that way. Sin has consequences: "For the wages of sin is death, but the gift of God is eternal life through Jesus Christ our Lord" (Romans 6:23).

A man named Nicodemus lived long ago. He knew we would all die, and he took time to consider his humanity. He went to a controversial teacher to visit with him about the frailty of his existence. This teacher told him, " 'I tell you the truth, no one can see the kingdom of God unless he is born again' " (John 3:3).

Nicodemus surely thought that this was a ridiculous notion. He questioned how a person could be reborn physically. The teacher explained He was speaking in abstract terms: "Flesh gives birth to flesh, but the Spirit gives birth to spirit. You should not be surprised at my saying 'You must be born again' " (John 3:6-7).

The teacher was Jesus Himself, and in the 16th verse of that chapter He paved the highway that leads to the redemption of the sin into which we are all born.

" 'For God so loved the world that he gave his one and only Son, that whoever believes in him shall not perish but have eternal life' " (John 3:16).

Abstract terms are fine but I have always considered myself a "where the rubber meets the road" kind of a guy. If you have any doubts about where you will spend eternity if your number were called today, the rubber meets the road in these verses:

...if you confess with your mouth, "Jesus is Lord," and believe in your heart that God raised him from the dead, you will be saved. For it is with your heart that you believe and are justified, and it is with your mouth that you confess and are saved.
                    -Romans 10:9-10

Take note: the Holy Scriptures do not mention race, age, gender, or denominational background. All are sinners and all can be saved!

Some of you may be a little skeptical. To those who are confused by the many different ideas floating around, this verse is for you. In John 14:6, Jesus declared, "I am the way and the truth and the life. No one comes to the Father except through me."

If you find what I have said to be the truth
and if you believe that Jesus is the Son of the living God,
that He came to earth for the redemption of mankind,
shouldered the sin of the world
and died on the cross for the remission of those sins,
that He rose again on the third day,
defeating death for all those who would believe,
for all time,
then know that you have the right to receive Him
and become a child of God.

Scripture assures us, "Yet to all who received him, to those who believed in his name, he gave the right to become children of God—" (John 1:12).

There is no special place or appointed time set aside for you to meet the Lord. You can do it right where you are, right now. In Revelation 3:20, Jesus promised, "Here I am! I stand at the door and knock. If anyone hears my voice and opens the door, I will come in and eat with him, and he with me."

If you have *any* doubts about where you will spend eternity, I invite you to say a little prayer:

Dear Lord Jesus,

I know that I am a sinner. I believe You died for my sins and then rose from the grave.

Right now, I turn from my sins and open the door of my heart and life.

I receive You as my personal Lord and Savior.

Thank You for saving me.

Amen.

Tell a believing friend and a pastor about your commitment. Or drop me a note in care of

The Hometown Missionary
P. O. Box 876
Waukee, IA 50263

About the Author

Danny Moon is a graduate of Lincoln High school in Des Moines, Iowa and a veteran of the United States Marine Corps. He is a graduate of the Iowa Department of Public Safety Academy and has served in law enforcement for the past 12 years. He currently is an accident investigator with the Iowa State Patrol and teaches accident investigation at the Academy as well as for other law enforcement agencies.

Danny's entering law enforcement and writing this book follow the same path: he was called to do each. His response has been to obey and take one step at a time.

He has studied the Bible through Moody Bible Institute and at Liberty University in Lynchburg, VA. He is currently enrolled in Berean University.

Danny and his high school sweetheart have been married for 15 years. They find great joy in raising their three children.

For information on ordering this book contact
The Hometown Missionary
P. O. Box 876
Waukee, IA 50263

http://showcase.netins.net/web/hmtwnmisonry

———————

If you have a personal "faith in daily life" experience you would like to share with the author, please send a printed copy of your own "hometown missionary" story along with your name, address, phone number, e-mail address, and current job position to

Faith Story
The Hometown Missionary
P. O. Box 876
Waukee, IA 50263

e-mail: themoons@netins.net